MW01127090

Mission

The *Community Literacy Journal* is an interdisciplinary journal that publishes both scholarly work that contributes to theories, methodologies, and research agendas and work by literacy workers, practitioners, and community literacy program staff. We are especially committed to presenting work done in collaboration between academics and community members, organizers, activists, teachers, and artists.

We understand "community literacy" as including multiple domains for literacy work extending beyond mainstream educational and work institutions. It can be found in programs devoted to adult education, early childhood education, reading initiatives, or work with marginalized populations. It can also be found in more informal, ad hoc projects, including creative writing, graffiti art, protest songwriting, and social media campaigns.

For us, literacy is defined as the realm where attention is paid not just to content or to knowledge but to the symbolic means by which it is represented and used. Thus, literacy refers not just to letters and to text but to other multimodal, technological, and embodied representations, as well. Community literacy is interdisciplinary and intersectional in nature, drawing from rhetoric and composition, communication, literacy studies, English studies, gender studies, race and ethnic studies, environmental studies, critical theory, linguistics, cultural studies, education, and more.

Subscriptions

Donations to the *CLJ* in any amount can be made with a check made out to "FIU English Department," with *Community Literacy Journal* in the memo line.

Send to:

> Paul Feigenbaum
> Department of English
> Florida International University
> DM462D
> 11200 SW 8th St.
> Miami, FL 33199

Donors at the $40 level or above will receive a courtesy print subscription of the academic year's issues.

Cover Artist and Art

Cover art provided by Ronnie Dukes.

> Within the white rectangular frame is the world represented in circular layers.

> The outermost circle is the American suburbs. Turbulent red and blue skies surround the green suburbs.

The inner circle within are the three branches of the American government—legislative, executive, and judicial. Surrounding the buildings of the three pillars of government are pallets of gold being guarded by a blue circle of police acting as a border. They are protecting the money from the inner city.

At the edge of the city are immigrants entering the United States via a broken wall. The rusty wall is broken by the golden scale of justice.

The small opening in the wall is a crack and water leaks through nurturing a growing plant beyond the feet of the immigrants. The water glows as it touches the plant. The small bright green plant seedling is on a black background.

The one plant represents the few who benefit from trickle-down economics and trickle-down justice.

Despite all the injustices and abuses, we will always find a way. This image represents growth and possibility despite the obstacles.

Submissions

Submissions for the Articles section of the journal should clearly demonstrate engagement with community literacy scholarship, particularly scholarship previously published in the *Community Literacy Journal*. The editors seek work that pushes the field forward in exciting and perhaps unexpected ways. Case studies, qualitative and/or quantitative research, conceptual articles, etc., ranging from 25-30 manuscript pages, are welcome. If deemed appropriate, we will send the manuscript out to readers for blind review. You can expect a report in approximately 10-12 weeks.

Community Literacy Journal is committed to inclusive citation practices and encourages authors to cite and acknowledge ideas of BIPOC scholars, activists, and organizers in community literacy.

The *Community Literacy Journal* also welcomes shorter manuscripts (10-15 pages) for three sections reviewed in-house:

Community Literacy Project and Program Profiles will discuss innovative and impactful community-based projects and programs that are grounded in best practices. We encourage community-based practitioners and non-profit staff to submit for this section. Profiles should draw on community literacy scholarship, but they are not expected to have the extended lit reviews that are customary in the articles section of the journal. If you are a community member wanting to submit, and it is your first time writing for an academic journal, we are happy to offer mentorship and answer questions. Pieces co-authored by multiple stakeholders in a project are also welcome.

Please submit using our online submission system. Contact the Project and Program Profiles Editor, Vincent Portillo, with questions at portilvi@bc.edu.

Issues in Community Literacy will offer targeted analysis, reflection, and/or complication of ongoing challenges associated with the work of community literacy. Potential subjects for this section include (but are not limited to): building/sustaining infrastructure, navigating institutional constraints, pursuing community literacy in graduate school, working with vulnerable populations, building ethical relationships, realizing reciprocity, and negotiating conflicts among partners. We imagine this as a space for practitioners to raise critical issues or offer a response to an issue raised in a previous volume of the *CLJ*.

We encourage community-based practitioners and non-profit staff to submit for this section. If you are a community member wanting to submit, and it is your first time writing for an academic journal, we are happy to offer mentorship and answer questions. Pieces co-authored by multiple stakeholders in a project are also welcome.

Please submit using our online submission system. Contact the Issues in Community Literacy Editor, Cayce Wicks, with questions at cwicks@fiu.edu.

Coda: Community Writing and Creative Work welcomes submissions of poetry, creative nonfiction, short stories, and multigenre work on any topics that have ensued from community writing projects. This may be work about community writing projects, and this may be expressed in ways we have yet to imagine. We ask authors to include a personal reflection about the submission itself—information about your community writing group (if you belong to one); your personal journey as a writer; what inspired you to write your piece; and anything else you'd care to share about your life—as an invitation for the author and Coda's readers to consider writing and activism as intertwined. Contact Coda editors with questions at Coda.Editors@gmail.com.

Authors interested in reviewing for the CLJ should contact Book and New Media Review Editor Jessica Shumake at jessica.shumake@gmail.com.

Advertising

Community Literacy Journal welcomes advertising. The journal is published twice annually, in the Fall and Spring (November and May). Deadlines for advertising are two months prior to publication (September and March).

Ad Sizes and Pricing

Half page (trim size 5.5 x 4.25): $200
Full page (trim size 5.5 x 8.5): $350
Inside back cover (trim size 5.5 x 8.5): $500
Inside front cover (trim size 5.5 x 8.5): $600

Format

We accept .PDF, .JPG, .TIF or .EPS. All advertising images should be camera-ready and have a resolution of 300 dpi. For more information, please contact Veronica House (housev@colorado.edu) and Paul Feigenbaum (pfeigenb@fiu.edu).

Community Literacy Journal is a member of the Council of Editors of Learned Journals.

Production and distribution managed by Parlor Press.

(CELJ)

Publication of the *Community Literacy Journal* is made possible through the generous support of the English Department and the Writing and Rhetoric Program at Florida International University. The *CLJ* is a journal of the Coalition for Community Writing. Current issues and archives are available open access at https://digitalcommons.fiu.edu/communityliteracy/

spring 2023

COMMUNITY LITERACY *Journal*

Editors	Isabel Baca, *The University of Texas at El Paso* Paul Feigenbaum, *Florida International University* Veronica House, *University of Denver*
Acquisitions Editor	Sherita Roundtree, *Towson University*
Senior Assistant Editor and Issues in Community Literacy Editor	Cayce Wicks, *Florida International University*
Journal Manager	Erin Daugherty, *University of Arkansas at Fayetteville*
Book and New Media Review Editor	Jessica Shumake, *University of Notre Dame*
Consulting Editor and Project Profiles Editor	Vincent Portillo, *Boston College*
Coda: Community Writing and Creative Work Editorial Collective	Kefaya Diab, *University of North Carolina at Charlotte* Chad Seader, *William Penn University* Alison Turner, *ACLS Leading Edge Fellow, Jackson, Mississippi* Stephanie Wade, *Stony Brook University*
Senior Copyeditor	Elvira Carrizal-Dukes, *University of Texas at El Paso*
Copyeditors	Walter Lucken IV, *Wayne State University* Christine Martorana, *Florida International University*

COMMUNITY LITERACY *journal*

Spring 2023
Volume 17, Issue 2

Issues in Community Literacy

Book and New Media Reviews

Coda

Editors' Introduction

Isabel Baca and Paul Feigenbaum, with
Vincent Portillo and Cayce Wicks

With the current issue of the *Community Literacy Journal*, we are pleased to welcome two scholars to our editorial team. Dr. Isabel Baca of the University of Texas at El Paso has taken a position as one of our journal Co-Editors, and Dr. Sherita Roundtree of Towson University is our new Acquisitions Editor.

The contents of the issue reflect the kinds of serendipitous moments that occur every now and then in journal editing, as when a section of an officially non-special issue almost feels like a special issue. This particular serendipity spotlights independently submitted pieces on public memory and the ethics of storytelling. In "**'You Call It Honor, We Call It Dishonor.' Counterstorytelling & Confederate Monuments in Isle of Wight County, Virginia,**" authors Brooke Covington, Chief Rosa Holmes Turner, and Julianne Bieron demonstrate how counterstorytelling functions in places of ordinary democracy. Through a case study of a public hearing regarding a local confederate monument in Isle of Wight County, Virginia, Covington, Holmes Turner, and Bieron illustrate how the use of storytelling supports citizens' interpretations of confederate monuments. Informed by critical race theory, and employing counterstorytelling as a methodology, these authors position storytelling as a practical form of racial countermemory, analyze citizens' narratives, and explore counterstories as "persuasive tools used by ordinary people to support their social justice aims." In addition, by engaging with counterstorytelling, Covington, Holmes Turner, and Bieron model collaboration and reciprocity in community-based scholarship.

Erin Brock Carlson explores how archival digital storytelling can develop students' understanding of place. In the article "**'I Have Always Loved West Virginia, But...': How Archival Projects Can Complicate, Build, and Reimagine Place-Based Literacies,**" Carlson describes an archival digital project between multimedia writing students and a local history center in West Virginia. Focusing on the Battle of Blair Mountain, an important event in labor history, Carlson argues that such digital projects "can lead students to place-based narratives that could be a source for increased levels of critical literacy and in turn, sustained political and material change." With the students' digital project, Carlson further conveys the value of archival research and the importance of ethical storytelling.

We also offer a retrospective on the first five years of the Writing Innovation Symposium (WIS), which has taken place annually at Marquette University in Milwaukee, Wisconsin since 2018. Spearheaded by WIS co-founder and "Chief Capacitator" Jenn Fishman, "**Capacitating Community: The Writing Innovation Symposium**" engages various questions about what it means to build community within a locally situated convening space that has over time extended its outreach to a more national stage. The engine of this showcase is a dialogic mélange of recollections, insights, and connections offered by twenty-nine WIS participants from both academic and nonacademic backgrounds. The piece concludes with Fishman's "narrative recipe" inviting readers to build their own small conference communities.

This issue's Project and Program Profile features Randi Gray Kristensen's piece **"JAMAL: Adult Literacy Decolonizing Knowledge and Activism in 1970s Jamaica."** In this profile, Kristensen describes the difficulties and disruptions that took place while developing and staging a community play with members of a poor and working-class Jamaican community. The article focuses on Jamaica Movement for the Advancement of Literacy (JAMAL), which sought to promote literacy amongst everyday Jamaicans through classes, playwriting, and stage performance. Kristensen builds upon the scholarship of Beverly Bell (*Walking on Fire*), arguing for the importance of exposing and resisting ongoing forces of colonization. Finally, Kristensen's profile adds to a growing body of scholarship that speaks to the needs of decolonizing knowledge within the field of Caribbean Studies.

For our Issues in Community Literacy section, we offer space for contributors to analyze, reflect, and/or complicate ongoing challenges associated with the work of community literacy. For this issue, contributors explore a range of concerns that include disability justice, payment for community writing, and queer zine publishing in the South. In our first piece, **"Rhetorical Considerations for *Missy*, an LGBTQ+ Zine at the University of Mississippi,"** Tyler Gillespie reflects on his experience working as an advisor for the University of Mississippi's "first creative publication for/by LGBTQ+ students and allies." Examining the zine's development through the lens of literary practices within LGBTQ+ communities, Gillespie aims to "add to conversations on the ways educators and other stakeholders can help such students create spaces for community-building and counterpublics in their localized contexts."

In the collaborative essay **"Payment in the Polity: Funded Community Writing Projects,"** Audrey Simango, Matthew Stadler, and Alison Turner explore how their role as RAES (Reader/Advisor/Editors) for the The GOAT PoL (The Geopolitical Open Atlas of The Polity of Literature) bring to light a complicated issue in community literacy: money. They delve into the intricacies surrounding the role of money in their work as RAEs and in other funded community-writing projects, and they explore how small payments to individual participants impact the community writing process. Using their experience with The GOAT PoL, the authors probe questions concerning power and privilege in community-engaged publishing and propose that the exchange of money could perhaps "deepen and enrich" the "polity of literature."

In the final piece of our Issues section, **"Access as Praxis: Navigating Spaces of Community Literacy in Graduate School,"** Millie Hizer reflects on her experience as a disabled graduate student navigating community literacy spaces. Hizer uses her lived experiences as a beginning framework for exploring the intersecting challenges that "graduate student labor conditions and a lack of institutional support" create to form "significant barriers for disabled graduate students looking to engage in community literacy projects." Building on "Ada Hubrig's theorization of *disability justice informed community literacy*," Hizer proposes an "access as praxis" approach, which seeks to bring "visibility to the barriers preventing disabled graduate students from meaningfully engaging in community engaged work." By presenting three unique perspectives on a range of concerns important to community literacy, this Issues section demonstrates the complexity of the affordances and constraints of community-engaged work.

Our Book and New Media Review section, edited by Jessica Shumake, includes three reviews of books that we believe will be of interest to readers of the journal. This issue also features our third publication of "Coda: Community Writing and Creative Work," as edited by Kefaya Diab, Chad Seader, Alison Turner, and Stephanie Wade.

Articles

"You Call It Honor, We Call It Dishonor." Counterstorytelling & Confederate Monuments in Isle of Wight County, Virginia

Brooke Covington, Chief Rosa Holmes Turner, and Julianne Bieron

Abstract

This essay considers how everyday citizens use counterstorytelling as a persuasive tactic in sites of ordinary democracy like public hearings. Specifically, we examine the counterstories and stock stories shared during a public hearing held in Isle of Wight County, Virginia to determine the future of a confederate monument that stood in front of the county's courthouse. By focusing closely on one particular counterstory, this essay considers counterstorytelling as a form of racial countermemory that challenges dominant narratives by centralizing social justice and anti-racism. The authors aim to contribute to understandings of storytelling and its role within sites of participatory democracy, particularly concerning debates over contested memory objects.

Keywords: counterstory, community, narrative, critical race theory, anti-racism, rhetoric, social justice

Introduction

Our research examines how monuments and memorials shape the public's memory of our shared past. More specifically, we examine one case study: the local confederate monument that stood in front of Isle of Wight County's courthouse from 1905 to 2021 and the controversy that ensued during deliberations concerning whether or not to relocate the monument. In light of this case, we ask: How do ordinary citizens use storytelling to support their interpretations of confederate monuments, and in turn, how do these memory objects shape the collective identity of the community? To engage these research questions, we examine the narratives used by citizens at the public hearing to support their position on what should happen to the monument (if anything). Our analysis is informed by critical race theory and its interdisciplinary method(ology) of "counterstorytelling," which highlights the dominant (stock) stories that organize our culture and the marginalized stories that run counter to those dominant interpretations. By focusing closely on one *coun-*

terstory told by Chief Rosa Holmes Turner, we demonstrate how counterstorytelling functions as a rhetorical strategy in efforts to displace confederate monuments. This research offers lessons to storytellers hoping to disrupt, disturb, and challenge master narratives propagated about the confederacy and the remaining relics of white supremacy within our country's memorial landscape. Moreover, by sharing this work among three co-authors (a local counterstoryteller, an undergraduate student, and an assistant professor), we model the type of collaborative work we call for.

Who We Are

In preparing this manuscript, the authors take seriously the impetus set forth by critical race theorists and counterstorytellers to disrupt traditional research paradigms, challenge dominant ideologies, and centralize the embodied and experiential knowledges of people of color (Delgado, Solórzano & Yosso, Martinez, and Faison & Condon). In this effort, we join scholars who are insistent on the importance of documenting the persistence of racism and acknowledging the ways in which a hegemonic culture of whiteness infects our personal and professional lives.

Rosa joins this project as Chief of the Warraskoyack Tribe at Mathomank (Mathomauk) Village—she is also a Native-born resident of Isle of Wight County and a descendant of countless trailblazing ancestors who helped to shape Isle of Wight County and America's history for centuries. Rosa was raised on the Rushmere Reservation, once known as the Warraskoyack Shire but now called Isle of Wight County, which is located on the James River and historic Lawne's Creek tributary (named for Sir Christopher Lawne, an early settler and colonizer of the Virginia Company, who arrived on the Marigold in May 1618). Rosa grew up on the oral storytelling and documented accounts of her ancestors and pioneers who inhabited the historic Mathomank (Mathomauk) Village, including historical figures like like John White (1593), Captain John Smith, (1607, 1608, 1610, 1611), and Indian Interpreters Reverend Thomas Baylye (1603-1681), John King (1600-1670), Robert Poole (1565-1622) and Thomas Hughes (1620). Deep knowledge of her ancestral past has enabled her to speak from a position of strength and authority about the systemic racism she's faced in her lifetime. As a person of color, Rosa witnesses both the short- and long-term effects of white colonization and the erasure of her people's histories, which has supported and fueled a form of paper genocide that nearly eradicated BIPOC histories from official archives, libraries, and textbooks for centuries. Historical events like the Discourse of Western Planting (Richard Hakluyt, 1593), the Indian Massacre (1622), the Articles of Peace (Powhatan Indian Treaty, 1646), the Act of Cohabitation (1688-90), the Virginia Emancipation Act, (Manumission, 1772), the War of 1812, the American Civil War (1861-1863), the Racial Integrity Act (1924 Walter Plecker), the Prohibition Act (1932-38), Jim Crow, the Isle of Wight Annexation of Rushmere to Smithfield (1970-72), the Virginia Marine Commission Jim Crow Policy Practices (1950-Present), and all other War eras have significantly imposed majoritarian narratives on people of color in Isle of Wight County for generations, resulting in defamation of character, enslavement, economic hardship, false imprisonment, loss of land, harsh and inhumane punishment, gentrification, vilification, and intentionally nullifying the importance of the Black and Indigenous histories that help shape her county and the United States of America. Rosa contends that the Civil War Era and the concerted efforts of all who idolize the confederate monuments to this failed chapter in America's history enforces and even encourages the degradation of society.

Rosa has been an advocate for the disenfranchised citizens of Isle of Wight and surrounding localities for over two decades as the founder of Rushmere Community Development Corporation. As heated national, state, and local debates regarding confederate statues, public monuments, and memorials intensified, Rosa knew the spirits of the ancestors were calling for justice through her, and she could no longer keep silent. Rosa counted the cost of her silence and chose to answer the clarion call to stand up as a person of color in leadership and to speak truth to power during the Isle of Wight County public hearing. The "Lost Cause" rhetoric has gone on long enough. After being contacted by Brooke to work on this project, Rosa again chose not to be silent.

Brooke Covington comes to this research as a straight, cisgendered, white woman who had the privilege of earning a PhD in Rhetoric and Writing Studies, which caters to her long-held interest in the rhetorics of public monuments and memorials. Born and raised in Richmond, Virginia, Brooke grew up next to monuments, streets, bridges, schools, and entire communities named after confederate soldiers and supporters. As a descendant of the confederate south, Brooke tries to reckon with her troubling ancestral past by challenging Lost Cause narratives and amplifying the marginalized stories that have gone unheard for too long. While Brooke recognizes that her whiteness enables her to practice a form of "privileged resistance" (O'Brien), she nevertheless agrees with Jill Reglin that "the need is critical for white women to talk out loud about social and racial injustice, as far as we are able to understand it" (121). Her work in Isle of Wight County began in August of 2020 when she moved to Newport News, Virginia (about 20 miles from Isle of Wight) and quickly learned of many confederate monument controversies unfolding across the Tidewater region. She began tracing these controversies and the tactics used by ordinary citizens to argue for or against the displacement of confederate memory objects, which eventually led to a research partnership with her student, Julianne.

Julianne Bieron entered the project first as a student interested in pursuing rhetorical analysis more intentionally as an undergraduate researcher. Brooke and Julianne applied for a summer fellowship opportunity to support undergraduate research projects and theirs focused exclusively on the confederate monument controversy in Isle of Wight County. Julianne grew up in Springfield, Virginia outside of Washington, DC. After living part-time in the Tidewater area of Virginia since 2016, she relocated full time in 2020 in the midst of the height of the Black Lives Matter movement. As a white woman living in a primarily Black community, she embarked on this research project to use her platform as a student of writing to support the voices of people of color in the Tidewater region.

Isle of Wight County, Virginia

The counterstory we later highlight was shared by Chief Rosa Holmes Turner on September 3, 2020 at a public hearing in Isle of Wight County, Virginia–a small rural county of approximately 39,000 residents located in the southeastern region of Virginia. According to 2020 U.S. Census data, the county demographics are 72.6% white, 23% Black, 4.7% Hispanic or Latinx, 2.8% two or more races, and 1.1% Asian (U.S. Census Bureau). Before sharing Rosa's story, the authors want to provide a little background on the Isle of Wight County confederate monument and the controversy faced by its residents.

Thanks to the fundraising efforts of the United Daughters of the Confederacy, the "Monument to the Confederate Dead" was erected in front of the Isle of Wight County courthouse on Memorial Day on May 30, 1905. According to the curators at the Isle of Wight County Museum, the statue itself was one of many mass-produced war memorials circulating at this time (England and Holtzclaw). Its features include a quadrangle staff situated on a hexagonal pedestal with inscriptions. On top of the pedestal is an unidentified confederate soldier, often called "Johnny Reb," wearing Confederate States of America military garb and holding a gun. Each of the six inscriptions is described in Appendix A.

Public concern over the presence of the monument in front of the courthouse reached a boiling point during the summer of 2020 as citizens witnessed a surge of racial reckoning in the U.S. The murders of George Floyd and Breonna Taylor at the hands of law enforcement officers led to a wave of Black Lives Matter protests across the nation, including in Isle of Wight County. Protestors and advocates lobbied for the systematic removal of confederate monuments from public spaces. Thanks to such efforts, state protections concerning memorials for war veterans in the state of Virginia were overturned in the summer of 2020.

Prior to July 1, 2020, the Code of Virginia (§15.2-1812) prohibited local authorities or individuals from removing, damaging, or defacing an established war memorial. After July 1, 2020, Virginia localities were granted the ability to erect, remove, relocate, contextualize, or cover any publicly owned monument. Like many other locales in the state of Virginia, Isle of Wight County found itself reconsidering the protection it once afforded the confederate monument that stood in front of its county courthouse. Pressure from local citizens in Isle of Wight County forced the county's Board of Supervisors to act–on July 16, 2020, Supervisor Rudolph Jefferson (the only person of color on the Board) proposed holding a public hearing to determine what (if anything) should be done with the monument. The public hearing was approved with a 4 - 1 vote and scheduled for a special session on September 3, 2020.

Isle of Wight County residents were invited to attend the in-person public hearing on September 3, 2020 or to submit email comments to the Board of Supervisors. Those present at the public hearing were asked to abide by specific guidelines when sharing their comments. Each citizen was asked to begin their comments by clearly stating their name, address, and electoral district of residence.[1] The Chair of the Board was emphatic that "the public hearing shall not serve as a form of debate with the Board or individual members of the Board," though citizens were asked to direct their comments only to the Board members, not the audience or the media. Each citizen was allotted 4 minutes to give comments, while any speaker who represented a group of 10 or more individuals was allotted 6 minutes to speak on behalf of the group.

Of those present at the public hearing, 48 people spoke, 21 in favor of removing the statue, and 27 against removal. Of the 147 unique citizen comments submitted via email to the Board of Supervisors, 42 were pro-removal and 105 were anti-removal. If the decision had been made solely based on numbers, it is likely that the confederate monument would still be standing at the county courthouse today. However, many of the comments (or, as we argue, the counterstories) offered by those in support of removing the monument persuaded the Board of Supervisors to take a different route.

By the end of the 4-hour long public hearing, the Board of Supervisors decided to forego a formal vote. Convinced that the most appropriate path forward was either relocation or contextualization (which involves adding informational signage, other statues, or educational materials to explain the history surrounding the monument), the Board instead created a Monument Taskforce of eight residents who were tasked with providing the Board recommendations for relocation and contextualization ideas. Though the Taskforce was unable to reach consensus, their recommendations to the Board ultimately resulted in the monument's relocation to private property owned by a local resident but granted to Isle of Wight County through an easement. County taxpayers paid $32,500 to remove and relocate the monument in April of 2021.

Because of the COVID-19 pandemic, the public hearing was live streamed via Facebook Live–which is how two of the authors–Brooke and Julianne–engaged with the public hearing. Rosa was present at the public hearing and spoke, in addition to emailing her story and photographs to the Board of Supervisors (see Appendix B for a full transcript of Rosa's testimony comments). In the next section, we more fully introduce critical race theory and its interdisciplinary method(ology) of counterstorytelling. From there, Rosa shares her emailed public hearing comments, and together, we explore how Rosa's comments function as a form of counterstorytelling.

Critical Race Theory & Counterstorytelling

We turn to critical race theory and its method(ology) of counterstorytelling to help us understand how narratives from the public hearing challenged the dominant ideologies and confederate rhetoric circulating in Isle of Wight about the monument and its function. Critical race theory emerged from critical legal studies–a movement in the 1970s that emphasized the role of racism in American law and sought reforms based on the premise that all legal interpretation is political and therefore never objective or neutral. Critical race theory aptly assumes if racism and oppression are present in American politics, then it is most certainly embedded in our legal system and beyond. Critical race theorists have thus pushed to expand this lens to move beyond law and policy by examining how power, racism, and hegemonic whiteness function across social institutions (including areas like education, healthcare, commerce, and technology). According to rhetoric and writing studies scholar Aja Y. Martinez, critical race theory "argues that ignoring racial difference maintains and perpetuates the status quo with all of its deeply institutionalized injustices to racial minorities and insists dismissing the importance of race is a way to guarantee that institutionalized and systematic racism continues and even prospers" (2022). Critical race theory is thus an effort to challenge the status quo by situating the experiences of people of color as central to understandings of racism and whiteness.

But, catering to an intersectional perspective, critical race theory acknowledges that racism is intertwined with other forms of oppression, and thus "works toward the elimination of racism as part of a larger goal of opposing or eliminating other forms of subordination based on gender, class, sexual orientation, language, and national origin" (Solórzano and Yosso 2002, 25). And while scholars have identified several key tenets of critical race theory, we draw primarily from Daniel Solórzano and Tara Yosso who have identified five key characteristics that constitute basic principles of thought concerning critical race theory. According to Solórzano and Yosso, critical race theory:

1. Situates race and racism as central to other forms of subordination.

2. Challenges dominant ideology, particularly concerning majoritarian narratives about objectivity, meritocracy, color blindness, race neutrality, and equal opportunity.

3. Is committed to social justice and the elimination of racism, sexism, and poverty and the empowering of subordinated minority groups.

4. Recognizes the experiential and embodied knowledge of people of color as legitimate and critical to understanding racism and "challenges traditional research paradigms, texts, and theories used to explain the experiences of people of color" (26).

5. Emphasizes a transdisciplinary perspective that builds on knowledge across disciplines and insists on analyzing race, racism, and whiteness within historical and contemporary contexts.

These five themes have been picked up by several critical race theory scholars and represent a challenge to dominant modes of scholarship and knowledge creation that reify hegemonic whiteness (see Martinez, 2016, 2020; Delgado, 1989; Delgado Bernal, 2002; Solórzano & Yosso, 2002). We share these five tenets in particular because they are central to our methodology of *counterstorytelling*.

One of the method(ologie)s to emerge from critical race theory is known as counterstorytelling. Critical race counterstory recognizes that the dominant group in society justifies its position and maintains its dominance through the sharing (and naturalization) of dominant narratives or "stock" stories. Stock stories are dangerous in the sense that the stories dominant groups often tell about American "progress" or "merit" or "neutrality" become so naturalized that they do not appear like stories at all. Once naturalized, stock stories may simply be accepted as truth. *Counterstories* are those stories told by minoritized groups to counter the accepted stock narratives.

How can you recognize a counterstory? Solórzano and Yosso argue that "a story becomes a counterstory when it begins to incorporate the five elements of critical race theory" (2002, 39).

Of course, counterstories can be put towards many different ends–but one of the early pioneers of counterstorytelling, Richard Delgado, reminds us that:

> Counterstories can quicken and engage conscience. Their graphic quality can stir imagination in ways in which more conventional discourse cannot. But stories and counterstories can serve an equally important destructive function. They can show that what we believe is ridiculous, self-serving, or cruel. They can show us the way out of the trap of unjustified exclusion. They can help us understand when it is time to reallocate power. They are the other half–the destructive half–of the creative dialectic. (2415)

Counterstorytelling is thus both a method *and* methodology–it can be the research tool (the instrument used to collect data) and/or the rationale and approach guiding the research process (the lens through which the data analysis occurs). Important for our purposes, "counterstorytelling recognizes that the experiential and embodied knowledge of people of color is legitimate and critical to understanding racism that is often well-disguised in the rhetoric of normalized structural values and practices" (Martinez 69). Thus, we bring this critical lens to the counterstories and stock stories shared at the public hearing in Isle of Wight County on September 3, 2020. Recognizing that Brooke and Julianne could not possibly understand the experiential or embodied knowledge shared by Rosa in her comments, the duo invited Rosa to join them as a co-author, co-creator, and co-researcher in hopes that we all might take seriously the challenge to disrupt traditional approaches to scholarly research; to privilege counterstorytelling in messy, emotional, and complicated real-world contexts; and to bear witness to the transformative power of storytelling as a tool of social justice and anti-racism.

Rosa's Counterstory

To avoid sterilizing the power of Rosa's counterstory, we quote her public hearing commentary in full–doing so is also an effort to avoid white-washing the narrative by forcing it into the linguistic code required of certain genres in academia. We chose to foreground Rosa's emailed comments, rather than her spoken testimony, because she directs the Board of Supervisors to her emailed comments in her public hearing testimony (Rosa's full public hearing testimony appears in Appendix B). The following is a direct transcript of the message Rosa sent to the Board of Supervisors ("Written Comments"):

Dear Board of Supervisors,

My family ancestors have been documented in this County for more than 12,000 years and today, I lift my voice to be heard on behalf of those I represent. I ask that the Isle of Wight County Board of Supervisors vote to remove the Confederate Statue from the Isle of Wight County complex on Monument Circle.

On 8/ 15/ 2020, as the Confederate monument was being removed from the public grounds at the Surry County Circuit Court House, I saw it as a victory and first step, to apologize for the inhumane treatment my Great -great Grandmother, Elizabeth Bailey-Howlett, (1837-1932), endured under the hands of a Confederate Soldier. Seated in the picture dressed in black, a FPOC (Free Person of Color), she was raped by a Confederate Soldier during the Civil war and left to die. By the grace of God, a Union Soldier rescued her and her family, thus allowing her legacy and future generations, like me, to be born.

My Big Daddy, (Grandfather), the late Pastor Harvey P. Johnson, was made to clear the ground where this statue sat, knowing that his wife 's grandmother had been raped and brutalized by a Confederate Soldier. He was paid $0.10 for performing his work assignment.

It's a bittersweet moment for me and my family. I pray that my Great -Great Grandmother's story and many others who endured the painful injustice inflicted on them during the Civil War era, as well as, any other era that focused on preserving slavery and oppression of another human race for their own selfish economic gain, should be told in the Local Government Chambers, Virginia General Assembly, United States Congress and Senate, and across this Nation.

Surry and Isle of Wight County are like Siamese twins that were separated at one point at their Lawnes Creek Vain. Just because they were separated does not mean they're not still connected. Twins always feel the hurt, joy, and pain of each other.

My Great -Great-Great Grandfather, John K. Claggett, was a staunch Confederate and a brutally hateful taskmaster, as our family's Oral history have shown. However, my Great -Great Grandfather, John C. Claggett, loved my Great Grandfather the late Robert W. Claggett, (1886 -1965), from his mixed-race intermarriage to Margaret Haskett , as well as, the rest of his children, Charles M., John H, Evelina, Queen Anne, and Sarah.

No one has ever glorified the person or unit who lost the war or came in 2nd place. No Isle of Wight County citizen should have to pay perpetually for a population who chose to uphold the right to enslave a people as if it was their God given right to do so.

My ancestors Thomas Hughes, Robert Claggett, Samuel Arthur Holmes, William Holmes, all served this Country and fought for freedom, not for the right to celebrate and preserve slavery throughout this County.

So Isle of Wight County, Board of Supervisors, please follow suit with your Siamese twin Surry County, and vote to take down your Confederate monument effective immediately.

It's time for our communities to heal from what is a constant reminder that our family members were beaten, enslaved, raped, tortured, and murdered, at the hands of many Confederate soldiers, whose descendants are still wreaking havoc over our children and family members today through Systemic Racism and Economic Disparity.

Sincerely,
Rosa Holmes Turner, Rushmere, Virginia
Chief of the Mathomank Village Tribe

Counterstory Analysis

In the following sections, we demonstrate how Rosa's counterstory confronts many of the features of the stock stories that were circulating at the public hearing. We focus our analysis on Solórzano and Yosso's five central tenets of critical race theory to draw the reader's attention to specific counterstorytelling persuasive tactics. Such rhetorical tactics are worthy of consideration, since it is through these counter-narratives that citizens of Isle of Wight County were able to convince the Board of Supervisors to act–and to act in a way that prioritized social justice and anti-racism, even though such actions largely went against the majority opinion.

Rosa begins her counterstory by directly asking the Board of Supervisors "to remove the Confederate Statue from the Isle of Wight County complex on Monument Circle." She continues, arguing that taking down the monument would be a way "to apologize for the inhumane treatment [of] my Great-great Grandmother, Elizabeth Bailey-Howlett (1837-1932)... [who] was raped by a Confederate Soldier during the Civil war and left to die. By the grace of God, a Union Soldier rescued her and her family, thus allowing her legacy and future generations, like me, to be born" ("Written Comments" para. 3). Unlike stock stories that often invite listeners to adopt the perspective of the oppressor, this counterstory invites listeners to adopt the perspective of those living with oppression. Here, we see Rosa inviting the listener to adopt the perspective of Elizabeth Bailey-Howlett–to bear witness to all the horror and trauma she experienced under the hands of the confederacy. By drawing from her great-great grandmother's experiential knowledge concerning confederate soldiers, Rosa is able to call into question stock stories that frame confederate soldiers as genteel heroes or even mere foot soldiers, protecting their lands and their state's rights.

In several ways, Rosa's testimony presents a case study in counterstory as a form of *racial countermemory*, as April O'Brien and James Chase Sanchez have theorized. According to O'Brien and Sanchez, racial countermemory is a marginalized form of remembering that "looks to identify, analyze, and refute dominant racial narratives and replace them with narratives that have either been forgotten or suppressed" (10). By sharing the counterstory of her great-great grandmother, Elizabeth Bailey-Howlett, Rosa presents a racial countermemory that refutes hegemonic Southern narratives of confederate soldiers as genteel defenders of the South and challenges the selective amnesia embedded in dominant historical narratives about the Confederacy. In this sense, her counterstory–as a form of racial countermemory, "disrupts and deconstructs [dominant historical narratives] by presenting a competing narrative of the same evidence, augmenting the narrative already in place with additional information, [and] telling the story from the perspective of a marginalized group" (O'Brien & Sanchez p. 9). Instead, Rosa demonstrates, through the embodied experiences of Elizabeth Bailey-Howlett, that these racial countermemories have been minimized, elided, and suppressed from Lost Cause ideologies in order to present confederate supporters as blameless in their so-called defense of the south.

Many stock storytellers leverage what Stephen Monroe dubs "confederate rhetoric," which appeals to the perspectives of the dominant group–in this case, white confederate ancestors. According to Monroe, "confederate rhetoric has played a formative role in creating and re-creating southern identities across time, slowed progress toward racial harmony, and reinforced racial barriers built by previous generations… it has performed this work while often obfuscating its purpose and protecting its existence" (5). These stock storytellers call on the Board of Supervisors "to stand up. Stand up for the over 100 men who died, did not return home from that war. Stand up for the thousands of descendants that they have here in this county, along with the 700 more people who served in that war" ("Special Meeting" Speaker 18). Such narratives are emblematic of the "magical thinking of the Lost Cause advocates, who emphasiz[e] the fact of the fighting, not its purpose or its consequence" (O'Neill 58). This stock storyteller only considers the perspective of the oppressive white majority; thereby ignoring and avoiding any responsibility to the nearly 4 million enslaved peoples whose freedom was at stake in this war. Instead, the implicit–and at times, explicit–argument made by these stock storytellers is that the "heroic" experiences of white confederate ancestors matter more than the experiences of BIPOC communities and their ancestors. Monroe explains that this is precisely how confederate rhetoric works:

> When white people defend or tolerate Old South words or symbols… they are in effect asserting cultural dominance over the parameters of public memory… such rhetorical ploys are nothing more than silencing methods… to shame, shun, and marginalize those in the Black minority–and their allies–who dare to forward public memories divergent from accepted, traditional, and white orthodoxies. (14–15).

For over 150 years, the Lost Cause has been built and sustained by these narratives, but counterstorytellers like Rosa commit to social justice by centralizing the often unheard stories of their ancestors, by elevating those stories that exist outside dominant narratives.

Rosa continues her story, describing her grandfather, "the late Pastor Harvey P. Johnson [who] was made to clear the ground where this statue sat, knowing that his wife's grandmother had been raped and brutalized by a confederate soldier" ("Written Comments" para. 4). This feature of Rosa's counterstory challenges stock storytellers who avoid responsibility for racism by foregrounding arguments about racial progress in the US. For example, one stock storyteller acknowledges that the monument was raised "at a time of Jim Crow and segregation, but America worked past that. We ended slavery. We have the civil rights movement that made great gains in the 1960s... the progress Black Americans have made in 150 years is remarkable" ("Special Meeting" Speaker 14). Though this stock storyteller does acknowledge the fact that the monument was raised during the height of the Jim Crow era, he fails to consider how or even why this monument might have functioned as a segregationist scare tactic positioned directly in front of the county courthouse. Instead, the teller opts to focus on the "great gains" made since segregation, thus situating race as a non-issue in America. Such racial progress narratives are comforting stock stories told by the dominant group to protect their privileged position and to avoid their own complacency within systems of injustice. Counterstories like Rosa's disrupt such comforting stock stories by highlighting the timelessness of racism and, in this case, pointing to the consistent racial injustices experienced across generations within Rosa's family.

In each of these examples, Rosa exhibits a key feature of critical race counterstory in that she draws from the experiential and embodied knowledges of her ancestors. She continues to practice this feature of counterstorytelling, even when it requires acknowledging her great-great-great grandfather, John K .Claggett, who "was a staunch Confederate and a brutally hateful taskmaster, as our family's Oral history have shown" ("Written Comments" para. 7). She continues, describing her "Great-Great Grandfather, John C. Claggett, [who] loved my Great Grandfather the late Robert W. Claggett, (1886-1965), [who was born] from his [John C's] mixed-race intermarriage to Margaret Haskett, as well as, the rest of his children, Charles M., John H, Evelina, Queen Anne, and Sarah" ("Written Comments" para. 7). In other words, Rosa's ancestral line in the 19th century includes *both* a Confederate taskmaster and an interracial marriage. What's significant here is that Rosa rejects stock stories that situate the importance of familial legacy or "heritage" before social justice by calling attention to her complex racial ancestry. Unlike "confederate rhetoric [which] has perpetuated the [over]simplification of racial categories of the US South" (Monroe 7), Rosa's experiential and embodied knowledge as a descendent of both white and Black southern ancestors disrupts the artificial Black/white binary promoted by confederate rhetoric. As Monroe explains, dominant narratives that emerge from the US South have consistently defined race in a binarism where a person is either white or Black. And this "false binary of race is one of the cornerstones of the South's comprehensive system to privilege white people and oppress Black people" (7). The hyperfocus on racial binaries serves to protect and unify white southerners by preserving racial divisions and (re)enforcing the racial order of the Old South. And yet, Rosa's very existence shatters the artificial Black/white binary confederate rhetoric so desperately aims to protect as a means of defending a (false) sense of white racial superiority.

In fact, Rosa models a way to acknowledge and reckon with ancestors who have upsetting or even intolerable histories. Such acknowledgement is in direct contrast to the confederate rhetoric promoted by stock storytellers who glorify ambiguous notions of "heritage" without critical or intentional consideration as to what that heritage might actually include. Indeed, defenses of confederate memory objects that appeal to "heritage not hate" rely on remembering by forgetting. Connor Towne O'Neill explains that "[t]his is what ideology does. We don't adapt our views based on the facts at hand, we assemble facts based on our ideology. We remember what we like. And white Americans are well practiced in this magical thinking, this selective memory" (115). Defenses like "heritage not hate" are vital fortifications in the defense of Isle of Wight as an island of and for whites. For example, one stock storyteller argued: "...that [the] monument is the closest thing to a tombstone those men will ever have… Now, people would have me disinherit or dishonor my great-great grandfather. I will not do that. I think he was a good man because his descendants were good people and I emulate some of their traits" ("Special Meeting" Speaker 18). Many of the Isle of Wight County citizens who spoke in favor of leaving the monument in front of the courthouse did so from this perspective–arguing that to remove the statue would be a dishonor to their noble confederate ancestors. Rosa–a descendant of a confederate taskmaster herself–thus embodies a direct challenge to perceptions of the confederacy and those who descended from its supporters. Indeed, Rosa invites listeners to consider whether ancestors with racist histories are deserving of honor.

Rosa is even more targeted in her spoken testimony to the Board, telling audiences, "My great-great grandfather John C. Claggett inter-married his black wife Margaret Haskett and they fought against the Confederacy, because they fought on the Union side" (2:43 - 2:44). This part of Rosa's story counters one of the main arguments made by stock storytellers, namely that the purpose of the monument was "only to commemorate soldiers that were [sic] sent by their government to fight a war, and were killed and buried on battlefields never to return" ("Special Meeting" Speaker 20). Many stock narratives attempt to present confederate soldiers as blameless men who were drafted and had little choice about which side to fight on. This pseudo-neutrality is called into question by Rosa's racial countermemory of her great-great grandfather, John C. Claggett, and great-great grandmother, Margaret Haskett, who both lived in the South but made the choice to fight in support of the Union and against the preservation of slavery.

Finally, this passage is also worth noting because Rosa purposefully draws the listener's attention to her family's oral histories–histories that have not been captured in any official capacity as a central part of the County's shared past. Similar to earlier passages, such a move is an intentional foregrounding of social justice, race, and the experiences of people of color. "Thomas Hughes, Robert Claggett, Samuel Arthur Holmes, William Holmes"–by saying their names, Rosa gives listeners a different set of historical figures, her family members, to draw histories from. Rather than prioritizing dominant stories about Jefferson Davis, Robert E. Lee, or even Abraham Lincoln in these debates, Rosa draws our attention to the lived realities of those who actually lived in Isle of Wight County before, during, and after the monument's residency at the courthouse.

Rosa ends her counterstory with one impassioned call:

> It's time for our communities to heal from what is a constant reminder that
> our family members were beaten, enslaved, raped, tortured, and murdered,

at the hands of many Confederate soldiers, whose descendants are still wreaking havoc over our children and family members today through Systemic Racism and Economic Disparity. ("Written Comments" para. 11)

This part of Rosa's counterstory is worth repeating because it features several of the key tenets of counterstorytelling. First, it demonstrates Rosa's unyielding commitment to social justice for those who were "beaten, enslaved, raped, tortured, and murdered at the hands of many Confederate soldiers" ("Written Comments" para. 11). Second, her appeal to the continued racism experienced by her ancestor's descendants, their family members, and their children is a direct challenge to racial progress narratives that attempt to present racism as a thing of the past from which we (Americans) have progressed beyond. But perhaps most importantly, Rosa's comment draws the listener's attention to the generational effects of racism and whiteness in the U.S. By doing so, Rosa's counterstory effectively situates issues of race and racism as not only central but *timeless*. This counterstorytelling persuasive tactic is in keeping with the principles of countermemory, since "countermemory is a way to link the past and the present instead of disassociating the present moment from the concerns of the past" (O'Brien & Sanchez p. 10). As Stephen Legg explains, countermemory reminds us of "the presentness of the past" (p. 186). While several stock storytellers situate racism within a context of bounded time (as a thing of the past), Rosa's comment challenges the listener to acknowledge the ongoing "presentness" of systemic injustices generated by racism and white supremacy since this country's founding.

Finally, we want to end our commentary by drawing the reader's attention to the middle of Rosa's testimony, where she writes, "...my Great-Great Grandmother's story and many others... should be told in the Local Government Chambers, Virginia General Assembly, United States Congress and Senate, and across this Nation" ("Written Comments" para. 5). Here, Rosa advocates for the transformative power of counterstorytelling as a form of racial countermemory and a tactic of resistance in sites of ordinary democracy. Indeed, this is a direct call to elevate the stories of those who exist outside of the dominant narrative–and this is a call we extend to our readers: *Listen to the counterstories. Tell the counterstories.*

Conclusion

This case study–and our collaborative analysis of it–contributes key insights across the fields of public memory studies, rhetorical studies, and critical race theory. We begin first by stressing what this article models: researchers need to actively center the situated knowledges of community actors in theories of counterstorytelling (and their practical applications). The same is true for scholarship that emerges from public memory studies since much of this work does not center community voices or community-based research methodologies like critical race theory's counterstorytelling. The analysis of this case study–collaboratively produced by 3 differently situated co-authors (an undergraduate student, and community member, and a faculty member)–models equitable research practices both within academia and the community. Our approach provides greater nuance in perspective and analysis than any one of us could provide alone. We are champions of this intentional work and advocate for other researchers to adopt similar approaches.

This piece also demonstrates that collaborative, reciprocal, community-based scholarship like ours plays a significant role in reshaping the way we think about and talk about race and public memory. Indeed, Rosa's counterstory as a racial counter-memory "exposes the fallacy of White America and compels [audiences] to grapple with a country built on inequality and injustice" (O'Brien & Sanchez p. 14). Such counterstorytelling "ask[s] us to contemplate our own lives, our own understandings of history, our own memories" (O'Brien & Sanchez p. 22). These countermemories and the curiosities they stir are vital to equitable and inclusive public memory/scapes.

In small rural communities like Isle of Wight County, the confederacy is so deeply embedded in the collective memory of some local residents that to attack it is to attack their history, their home, them. And yet we hope those reading whose ideologies align more closely with confederate stock stories are still open to hearing Rosa's counterstory–to reckon with and acknowledge her and her ancestors' histories. Those who remain closed to such counterstories are missing an important opportunity to practice what Bradford Vivian calls "commonplace witnessing" across ideological divides, to join friend and foe in bearing witness to historical tragedies or injustices in ways that can be therapeutic and reconciliatory for all.

This point leads to the next practical implication of this study: we, the authors, actively seek to change the national conversation regarding confederate monuments and critical race theory. We purposefully defined and applied critical race theory to a confederate monument within an open-access publication that is accessible to the general public and inclusive of academic and community perspectives. In doing so, we aim to disrupt baseless attacks against critical race theory as "racist" or "unpatriotic" or teaching white children to hate themselves. Instead, critical race theory is an effort to draw attention to the ways in which systemic racism has and continues to infect all aspects of society, including education, healthcare, law, housing, voting, memory, and every other aspect of American society. This article demonstrates how to practice "commonplace witnessing" of historical tragedies and injustices; how to promote a more inclusive, more equitable public memory; and how to face the lie of white supremacy through which America birthed and built a nation. Those who reject critical race theory without close and careful study of its tenets are avoiding cross-racial solidarity and progress in favor of the status quo–a state that has never been kind, much less inclusive or equitable to minoritized groups.

Beyond the methodological and practical implications of this case study, Rosa's counterstory also situates storytelling as a viable form of racial countermemory within the field of public memory studies, and counterstories such as these require greater attention from public memory scholars, especially due to the paper genocide Rosa describes in her introductory positionality remarks. Researchers who study objects of public memory must look beyond the statues and the archives to inform their analyses. A particularly apt place to locate counterstories that function as discursive and embodied racial countermemories include sites of active democratic deliberation, like public hearings.

In light of stock storytellers who claim that "many of us have never thought a day in our lives about confederate statues until the media put our focus on them" ("Special Meeting" Speaker 25), Rosa's counterstory is an important rejection of such thinking. Her comments make clear to listeners that if you "have never thought a day in [your life] about confederate statues," then you are likely a member of the white privileged majority. Such thinking is made even more apparent in whose perspective is included and excluded in pronouns such as "we" and "us" and "our" (regardless of whether these pronouns are used in a small town public hearing or an academic text). In other words, the constitutive power of rhetoric and the strategic use of pronouns enforce and enact racism and whiteness through whose perspective is included and whose is erased.

What this close exploration of Rosa's counterstory reveals is that counterstories are persuasive tools used by ordinary people to support their social justice aims. And while in this case, the transformative potential of storytelling led to the end of a confederate monument's 115-year residency in front of a county courthouse, in states like California, BIPOC families are tapping into the transformative power of countersto-rytelling to argue for the return of ancestral lands stolen during moments of racial terrorism in the US. Indeed, a few months after Isle of Wight County displaced its confederate monument, California lawmakers voted unanimously to return ancestral homelands that were taken from the Bruce family nearly 100 years ago, after their ancestors were run out of the area by Ku Klux Klan members and white neighbors. The reclamation of Bruce's Beach is inspiring other counterstorytellers across the US to argue for the reclamation of ancestral homelands lost to white supremacy and hatred.

It's stories like these that gives us hope. Perhaps Richard Delgado says it best when he writes, "Stories humanize us. They emphasize our differences in ways that can ultimately bring us closer together. They allow us to see how the world looks from behind someone else's spectacles. They challenge us to wipe off our own lenses and ask, 'Could I have been overlooking something all along?'" (2440). To unpack the full potential of counterstorytelling as a transformative critical race method(ology), rhetoricians must attune to the complex and textured narratives that everyday countersto-rytellers craft to support their persuasive ends, particularly within democratic contexts, like public hearings.

But to do this work well, academicians must not only expand what counts as research, but also look to different types of authors whose situated knowledges can (and should) be brought into the conversation. In fact, the hierarchy of who/what matters or who/what counts in scholarly research is in and of itself a stock narrative that researchers must reject, particularly when conducting research situated within communities. Rhetoricians who take seriously the challenge to study public counterstories as a form of racial countermemory must be willing to do this work alongside counter-storytellers in reciprocal and respectful ways. Otherwise, scholars risk colonizing the very narratives they/we hope to amplify. In her chapter from *Counterstories from the Writing Center*, Talisha Haltiwanger Morrison warns against this temptation to colonize. She notes that although advocacy for anti-racism in the academy is growing, there continues to exist "white scholars [who] are interested in speaking about rac-

ism, [who] have not made significant efforts to draw in the voices of those most affected by it" (Morrison 41). By actively including Rosa's voice and mind–to be guided
by her perspectives and her stories–we try to co-create knowledge, build trust, and
practice reciprocity. Our voices are louder together.

Here, we have tried to demonstrate the ways in which counterstorytelling functions in places of ordinary democracy, but there is more work to be done. Future research on the persuasive tactics employed during public hearings and other forms of
deliberative democracy can be enriched by a focus on counterstorytelling. Theories of
counterstorytelling also provide a useful framework for those who study public memory and the ways in which stock/counternarratives contribute to shared understandings of our collective pasts. In addition to more work that examines counterstorytelling as a form of racial countermemory, researchers should also consider examining
white resistance to counterstories and racial countermemories that recast confederate
symbols and challenge hegemonic Southern narratives.

One specific area we'd like to explore in future research concerns the embodied
dimension of counterstorytelling. How does counterstorytelling function as an embodied performance of social justice in sites of ordinary democracy? How are counterstorytelling performances impacted by codes of decorum (or even intentional in-
decorum), style, body language, clothing and accessories, among others? These lines
of inquiry will help expand understandings of counterstorytelling and its ability to
imagine a world otherwise. Nevertheless, we urge scholars to consider how to incorporate diverse perspectives into their counterstorytelling work–to draw from those
(counter)storytellers who exist beyond the ivory tower and therefore grapple differently with the social, cultural, and economic effects of race, racism, and whiteness
each day.

Notes

1. One of the anti-removal emails collected by the Isle of Wight Board of Supervisors was sent by a citizen present at the public hearing. He expressed his fear of re-
taliation against his family if he provided his address. The 22nd speaker at the public
hearing, a Black citizen of Isle of Wight in favor of removal, also acknowledged the
dangers minority people could face by providing their home addresses, but stated that
it was worth the risk.

Appendix A. Inscriptions on the Monument

Side #1:

ISLE OF WIGHT'S LOVING/
TRIBUTE,/
TO HER HEROES OF/
1861 TO 1865./
"THEY BRAVELY
FOUGHT,/
THEY BRAVELY FELL,/
THEY WORE THE GRAY,/
THEY WORE IT WELL."

Side #2

BRIGHT WERE THE LIVES/
THEY GAVE FOR US;/
THE LAND THEY STRUG-/
GLED TO SAVE FOR US,/
WILL NOT FORGET/
ITS WARRIORS YET,/
WHO SLEEP IN SO MANY/
GRAVES FOR US./

Side #3

THEY BLEED – WE WEEP/
WE LIVE– THEY SLEEP.

Side #4:

"THERE IS A TRUE GLORY/
AND A TRUE HONOR/
THE GLORY OF DUTY
DONE/
THE HONOR OF THE IN-
TEGRITY/
OF PRINCIPLE"

Side #5

"GLORIOUS IS HIS FATE,/
AND ENVIED IS HIS LOT,/
WHO FOR HIS COUNTRY/
FIGHTS AND FOR IT DIES."

Side #6

DEDICATED MAY 30, 1905

[Features an etching of an
American flag crossed with a
Confederate States of Amer-
ica flag]

Appendix B. Chief Rosa Holmes Turner Public Hearing Testimony

2:42:24 Rosa Holmes Turner. [ADDRESS REDACTED]. Hardy district. Rushmere was named in 1582, 35 years before Captain John Smith got here. So I just want to talk to you about my ancestors and my history with the confederacy. My ancestors have documented over 12,000 years here in Rushmere, and also in Isle of Wight County. And I just want to go through just some things. You all have a written document and I already told Mr Jones that I won't go through the whole document, and I will add one more document to that, but I just want to highlight some things.

2:43:01 First of all when you talk about the statue, yes I want you to vote to remove it from off of the government grounds where my taxes help pay for. So yes I do want you to move that. One of the reasons why is because when I see the Confederate statue and you have a picture… because this country and this state worked very hard to find individuals between 1800 and when photography and audio came to point, they wanted to make sure that they could preserve the history and those that have been enslaved and those that were attacked by the Confederacy.

2:43:38 You have a picture in your file, and is my great great grandmother, which is Elizabeth Bailey Howlett, who was raped by a Confederate soldier during the war. She was raped and left and her family were left for dead and it was a Union soldier that rescued her and her family so that I'm here to talk to you today on her behalf.

2:43:59 I want the statue removed off my property. The other thing I want you to know, I'm a blended remnant of Isle of Wight County. Not just the Native American, the Black American, but also my great great grandfather, my great great great grandfather, John K. Claggett was a Confederate taskmaster in Rushmere, Virginia. Very hard taskmaster in Rushmere, Virginia. With my great great grandfather John C. Claggett inter-married his black wife Margaret Haskett and they fought against the Confederacy, because they fought on the Union side.

2:44:42 And when we look at even not just the statue, that I want you all to remove off our our county property that our taxes pay for, I also want you to look at renaming Fort Huger the street. We've already given you Fort Huger the fort that was consumed within hours by the Union. Not just by the ironclad ships that were out in the water, but by the soldiers that my ancestors allowed, the foot soldiers for the Union, to march across their land in Rushmere to consume that Fort Huger. So your Honor, um, General Huger but we honor Thomas Hughes and others that fought to make sure that our people stayed safe.

2:45:23 Yes it's about ending slavery. Yes it's about oppression. Yes it stands for everything that you say. And I- I just want you to know that that it stands for that, not only that my Big Daddy, as we call it, Reverend Harvey Johnson was paid 10 cents to clear the land with some of these Confederate statues go and stand right now. The one in Surry County was moved. He told us the story of him having to clean that land that he knew that is great- that his grandmother-in-law had been raped by a confederate soldier.

2:45:56 So you call it honor, we call it dishonor. [overlapping applause] We call it un-repented dishonor because you never apologized. This county and everything else. Again we want to talk about the history that's documented for the Confederacy, the Confederate soldiers, well our Black free men of color helped build Fort Huger this county didn't even want to ever even pay. Virginia didn't want to pay them for the work that they did to do Fort Huger and it had to be somebody from Isle of Wight county that sent a letter to ask "what you want us to do with them? Do you want us to pay them or what."

2:46:31 Again oppression because you think it's for us to work for free on the properties that we have here that we pay taxes for and that we can't even get paid for the work that we do. Remove the statue off of our property that we pay to maintain in public works. Remove it from our other thing I want you to know–

[Off-screen, Board of Supervisor] Please bring yours to a conclusion.

[Rosa con't] Yes I will. I'll bring it to close. Finally, I just want you to know that we, we support that you remove the statue in an honorable way. Put it somewhere where they can reference and honor their, their soldiers and their fallen soldiers. But when we erect statues that we want to erect we assure you it's going to be on private proper-ty that we pay for with our own money, and not with the taxes that we ask this county to pay for. Thank you for your time.

[Applause]

Works Cited

Bernal, Dolores Delgado. "Critical Race Theory, Latino Critical Theory, and Critical Raced-Gendered Epistemologies: Recognizing Students of Color as Holders and Creators of Knowledge." Qualitative Inquiry, vol 8, no. 1, 2002, pp. 105-126.

Delgado, Richard. "Storytelling for Oppositionists and Others: A Plea for Narrative," *Michigan Law Review*, vol. 87, no. 8, 1989, pp. 2411-2441.

England, Jennifer and Mike Holtzclaw. Personal interview. 11 March 2021.

Faison, Wonderful, and Frankie Condon, editors. *Counterstories from the Writing Center*. Utah State University Press, 2022.

"Isle of Wight County Board of Supervisors. Special Meeting of the Isle of Wight County Board of Supervisors. Facebook Live. 3 September 2020. https://fb.watch/emxx3qbUSW/.

Isle of Wight County Board of Supervisors. Written Comments for 9-3-20 Confederate Monument Public Hrg. 3 September 2020. Access Date: 25 February 2021.

Legg, Stephen. "Sites of Counter-Memory: The Refusal to Forget and the Nationalist Struggle in Colonial Delhi." *Historical Geography*, vol. 33, pp. 180-201.

Martinez, Aja Y. "Council on Basic Writing Workshop: Keynote on the Craft of Counterstory." *Conference on College Composition and Communication*, 9 March 2022, Virtual.

Martinez, Aja Y. "A Plea for Critical Race Theory Counterstory: Stock Story vs. Counterstory Dialogues Concerning Alejandra's "Fit" in the Academy" in *Performing Antiracist Pedagogy in Rhetoric, Writing, and Communication*. eds. Frankie Condon and Vershawn Ashanti Young. WAC Clearinghouse, 2016.

Martinez, Aja Y. *Counterstory: The Rhetoric and Writing of Critical Race Theory*. 2020. Print.

Monroe, Stephen M. *Heritage and Hate: Old South Rhetoric at Southern Universities*. 2021. Print.

Morrison, Talisha Haltiwanger. "Beyond the Binary: Revealing a Continuum of Racism in Writing Center Theory and Practice" in *Counterstories from the Writing Center*. Eds. Wonderful Faison and Frankie Condon. Utah State University Press, 2022, pp. 35 - 43.

O'Brien, April and James Chase Sanchez. "Racial Countermemory: Tourism, Spatial Design, and Hegemonic Remembering." *The Journal of Multimodal Rhetorics*, vol. 5, no. 2, 2021.

O'Brien, Eileen. *Whites Confront Racism: Antiracists and their Paths to Action*. Lanham, MD: Rowman & Littlefield, 2001.

O'Neill, Connor Towne. *Down Along with that Devil's Bones: A Reckoning with Monuments, Memory, and the Legacy of White Supremacy*. 2020. Print.

Reglin, Jill. 2002. "A Long Path to Semi-Woke," in *Counterstories from the Writing Center*. eds. Wonderful Faison and Frankie Condon. Utah State University Press, 2022, pp. 120-132.

Solórzano, Daniel G., and Tara J. Yosso. "Critical Race Methodology: Counter-Storytelling as an Analytical Framework for Education Research." *Qualitative Inquiry*, vol. 8, no. 1, Feb. 2002, pp. 23–44.

U.S. Census Bureau. Population Estimates for Isle of Wight County, Virginia, April 2020. https://www.census.gov/quickfacts/isleofwightcountyvirginia (June 2021).

Author Bios:

Brooke Covington is an assistant professor in the Department of English at Christopher Newport University in Newport News, Virginia. As the Academic Director of CNU's Center for Community Engagement, Brooke is committed to the study and practice of anti-racist community engagement, and she was awarded a 2022 HuMetricsHSS Community Fellowship to support her efforts in this vein. Her research examines the rhetorics of public memory, particularly in relation to the ways in which audiences interpret and debate the form, function, and meaning of contested memory sites. Brooke holds a Ph.D. in Rhetoric & Writing from Virginia Tech, and her work has appeared in *Western Journal of Communication*, *Journal of Curriculum and Pedagogy*, *Journal of Medical Humanities*, and Campus Compact.

Chief Rosa Holmes Turner was born in Rushmere, Virginia, where she is now Chief of the Warraskoyack Tribe at Mathomank (Mathomauk) Village. Rosa earned a Bachelor of Science Degree in Design Technology & Industrial Management from Norfolk State University and an Executive Master's Certification in Global Business Leadership and Public Administration from Duke University Fuqua School of Business. She is currently pursuing a Master of Theology degree at the Samuel DeWitt Proctor School of Theology from Virginia Union University. She has served over 20 years in community development and outreach, both locally and nationally, through her non-profit, Rushmere Community Develop Corporation. Rosa became a licensed preacher in April 2022 at First Gravel Hill Baptist Church, under the leadership of Reverend Alexander Bracey, III. She is the author of two books, *The Remnant Story of the Warraskoyack Indians* and *Get Your House in Order, No More Chicken Dinner Funerals*.

Julianne Bieron graduated from the Honors Program at Christopher Newport University in December 2022 with a degree in English, concentrated in Writing. While at CNU, Julianne focused her research on topics that combined storytelling and social justice, including research on both Tolkien and Fan studies. She currently works in the excess and surplus insurance industry while continuing to produce creative writing with a focus on disability advocacy.

"I Have Always Loved West Virginia, But…": How Archival Projects Can Complicate, Build, and Reimagine Place-Based Literacies

Erin Brock Carlson

Abstract

This article shares the outcomes of a collaborative project between multimedia writing students and a local history center in which students created online exhibits about an important event in labor history: the Battle of Blair Mountain. The main outcome discussed is the enhancement of place-based literacy, including complication of simplistic narratives about place, illumination of less visible stakeholders, deeper understanding of hidden identity markers, and contextualization of relationships between artifacts and personal histories. Ultimately, this article demonstrates the value of archival research and the stories such research unveils as a means to re-imagine places and their people in more ethical, nuanced representations.

Keywords: Place-based literacy, archive, digital, storytelling, narrative, Blair Mountain

Place matters. This might seem like an obvious statement, but place is one of those factors that fades into the background seemingly just as often as it takes center stage. What might be less obvious is that when a place *does* receive attention, that place is oftentimes presented in one dimension. Overly simplistic renderings of places oftentimes reify monolithic narratives that perpetuate negative and inaccurate stereotypes that directly affect community members and their attitudes toward their own places. We see this dynamic unfold through vast generalizations about the differences between urban or rural communities, red or blue states, coastal or middle American regions, and so on—generalizations often crafted at the hands of media, entertainment, and political actors that don't reside in the areas being described.

One example of such a place is the state of West Virginia. From the much-embellished Hatfield-McCoy feud of the 1800s that paints West Virginians as territorial clans living in the backwoods to more recent cable news representations of West Virginia as the headquarters of "Trump Country," West Virginia has long been defined by those outside of the state. Stock stories (Martinez) and master narratives (Lyotard), or accounts that lack nuance in favor of clean, simplistic roles and actions, are powerful because we tend to lean on those narratives to quickly understand the world around us; however, clinging to those narratives obscures the presence of other stories that illuminate the complexities of places and people. These other, more complicated stories, or "little narratives...offer valuable insights...by providing alternatives to the dominant narratives often emphasized" (Alexander 612). Little narratives demonstrate the paucity of dominant narratives and offer people the capacity to challenge those dominant narratives in ways that complicate their understandings of themselves and their places.

Very rarely do stories embedded in pop culture and news media cast West Virginia in a positive light, but the state's history is filled with stories that paint a vastly different picture. One story is that of the Battle of Blair Mountain, which is, to date, the largest labor uprising in United States history. In the 1920s, a diverse coalition of coal miners—immigrants from Eastern Europe, Black workers who immigrated from the South, and white West Virginians—organized to demand better working conditions and subsequently faced violence from coal company forces. Though the miners lost that specific conflict, the event is seen as a significant event in labor history because it demonstrated the power of diverse coalitions across identity groups, and it ultimately led to major industry reforms. Blair Mountain challenges monolithic representations of West Virginia that cast it as backwards and overly conservative, offering a more complex portrayal of a place and its people that reaches back to the early 20th century. Such a portrayal is a direct confrontation against much of the discourse that circulates about West Virginians' home communities, as it signifies the power of seeking out little narratives.

In my role at a land-grant institution in West Virginia, I work with students from the state and surrounding areas, and one-dimensional narratives often find surface in our classrooms. In my work, I often witness students' perspectives on their places shift as they move from accepting dominant narratives to rejecting those stories to seeking ways to articulate *their* experiences in their own words–experiences that paint a vastly different picture of West Virginia from the stereotypes depicted in media. In writing classrooms, we can design assignments that help students make sense of these conflicting narratives and even to uncover previously unknown-to-them narratives that ultimately encourage students to craft more nuanced understandings of their places and of themselves. Because place both holds significant cultural meaning and is inherently relational (Fagerjord), place offers an important entry point into larger conversations about other issues in our writing classes, including power and privilege. And while this piece focuses on West Virginia, I want to note that many places are framed by external forces according to perceived deficits or weaknesses and I call on others to consider how their own place-based literacy work engages these tensions.

In Spring 2021, in anticipation of the 100th anniversary of the Battle of Blair Mountain, students in both sections of a course I teach entitled "Multimedia Writing" partnered with the West Virginia and Regional History Center to create online exhibits about the battle and events leading up to it. This organization is dedicated to preserving and sharing the history and culture of West Virginia and surrounding areas. Building on previous collaborations between myself and the Center (discussed later in this piece), students were tasked with building narratives to contextualize archival materials that document the battle, including photographs, journal entries, pamphlets, and physical objects, and then to share those narratives through online exhibits featured on the organization's website celebrating the anniversary. In their digital storytelling projects, students assembled intriguing counternarratives about the state even as they grappled with the complexities of displaying century-old, localized artifacts on 21st-century digital platforms.

In this piece, I demonstrate that digital storytelling projects that incorporate archival materials can support students as they develop deep understandings of place that might potentially empower students from often marginalized and misrepresented places. First, I draw on current discussions in literacy and writing studies to articulate the ways that working with place-based artifacts can help students reimagine the places they inhabit in meaningful ways, and I provide background on the Battle of Blair Mountain. This is followed by a description of the institutional context of the pedagogical project described in this piece. Next, I analyze the project's outcomes, including the ways that narratives about place were disrupted and reimagined as students built online exhibits about one of the most significant events in U.S. labor history. Finally, I conclude by arguing that archival, digital projects can lead students to place-based narratives that could be a source for increased levels of critical literacy and in turn, sustained political and material change.

Diving into place in the writing classroom with Blair Mountain

Place is simultaneously a shared and deeply personal phenomenon: we find kinship with those who share our places, embracing similarities and forming attachments in our hometowns and beyond; at the same time, the ways that we perceive a place depend on our own individual identities and past experiences. In the project described in this article, for example, students originally from West Virginia had different perceptions of the state and its history than their peers from surrounding states, as well as different levels of attachment to the events we discussed; however, this project provided everyone, regardless of background, with a more nuanced understanding of the state and its history. Writing teachers are no stranger to bringing narratives about place into the classroom, as illustrated by work surrounding ecocomposition (see Weisser and Dobrin), location-based digital media (see McNely; Rivers), and experiences in both urban and rural settings (see Donehower, Hogg, and Schell; Flower; and Long, respectively).

Carlo emphatically claims that "place is central to literacy practices and our theories about those practices" (68); again, place matters. And since place is a constant presence that shapes our experiences, incorporating attention to place in our writing classrooms can help us to better understand "how spaces impact upon learning, reading, and writing" and in turn, to better understand "difference, otherness, and the politics of exclusion—topics that define the causes of critical literacy, social justice, and liberatory education" (Reynolds 3). Gruenewald similarly links place to critical literacy, arguing that place-based methods of education require us to "explicitly examine the place-specific nexus between environment, culture, and education" (10). Donehower, Hogg, and Schell write that literacy skills are material in nature, and these skills can help people in particular areas "sustain life" when those skills are developed with that specific place in mind (4). An awareness of place fosters action by illuminating the complexities of place. In this piece, I describe place-based literacy as the skills that allow us to closely read texts that present differing or even conflicting narratives about a place, and then, to put those narratives into conversation with one another in meaningful and nuanced ways.

As such, place-based literacy requires an openness towards multiple accounts in order to avoid privileging one-dimensional master narratives over a "contextualized little narrative that challenges, contradicts, or even confirms" the overarching narrative (Alexander 623). Attention to place invites nuanced understandings of how we see not only our surroundings, but ourselves and those around us. By illuminating different stories, a place-based approach in the writing classroom offers students the opportunity to reimagine their surroundings. Gruenwald argues that pedagogies infused with place "ultimately encourage teachers and students to reinhabit their places, that is, to pursue the kind of social action that improves the social and ecological life of places, near and far, now and in the future" (7). In our classrooms, we can use writing to reinhabit places, whether that writing is used to redefine our own feelings towards a place or to foster change in our surrounding communities. Carlo explicitly links writing pedagogy and place-based literacy through the act of revision: "...when places are being revised, there is an impulse...to *conserve*–the land, the culture, the local businesses, the local residents–and there is an impulse...to *transform*, to make social reality better for those who have been traditionally marginalized or displaced (whether we are considering place as institution, place as neighborhood, place as city, or place as region)" (60). This act of revision can bring about deeply felt changes in students, especially those with roots in or connections to places that have been largely stereotyped by popular narratives.

Notions of place, then, are dynamic, not static; because place can harbor deep emotional or affectual meanings, our orientations toward them can change. Reynolds describes these meanings as "a swirling combination of metaphor and materiality" that we "carry...around with us in every encounter with a place" (175). Herndl et al. echo this understanding of how place and feeling intertwine, writing that a place has "a material and affective reality that can be seen, felt, and loved" (71). To tap into or to disrupt this reality is a way that writing instructors can encourage students to seek out multiple stories, to interrogate those narratives and their impacts, and to go forth with more nuanced understandings of place that they can then leverage in their own communities. This increased sense of place-based literacy can be especially powerful for students from marginalized places, rural and urban alike. In the introduction to their edited collection on Appalachian literacies, Webb-Sunderhaus and Donehower explicitly note the value of "uses of literacy that resist internal as well as external cultural forces...that continually resist and reshape the local, the nonlocal, and the relationships between the two" (8). Seeking out little narratives (Alexander) offers students the opportunity to reimagine their places in empowering ways.

The Appalachian region, which includes all of West Virginia, has a long history of stereotypical representation. These representations are rooted deeply in the national imagination, starting in the 1800s with "local color" newspaper articles and book bindings that depicted the region "as an undiscovered country filled to the brim with exotic creatures" (Plein 104). More recent examples, bolstered by J.D. Vance's popular memoir *Hillbilly Elegy* and a Netflix film of the same name, reify those perceptions that cast Appalachian people as backwards and lazy. But scholars in rhetoric and literacy studies have confronted these stereotypes. Webb-Sunderhaus notes the gap between stories of "hillbillies, rednecks, and white trash" and her own experiences as an Appalachian (5). Kurlinkus and Kurlinkus point to rhetorical appeals to a cultural nostalgia that paints the region in a monolithic and inaccurate light (88). And Hayes challenges the region's link to "illiteracy or outright hostility toward education" (72) by illuminating Appalachians' keen understanding of place and its impact on cultural knowledge.

Furthermore, as with any place, the dominant narrative is not the only narrative—and there are many stories of West Virginia that challenge stereotypes that seem so tightly held, including the Battle of Blair Mountain. As part of the Mine Wars (a series of conflicts between coal miners and coal companies in the early 20th century), Blair Mountain represents the culmination of decades of exploitation and intimidation in the West Virginia coal fields. One often-overlooked aspect of this time is the diversity of the workforce in the coal fields. In addition to born-and-bred West Virginians, European immigrants and African Americans from the South moved to the state for employment. Once they arrived, miners lived in company housing and shopped at company stores (with inflated prices) even as they received company wages, resulting in severe economic exploitation. This dynamic, combined with unsafe working environments, racial segregation forced by company representatives, and measures put in place to prevent workers from unionizing, led to unrest. Regarding central and southern West Virginia in the early 20th century, Humphreys et al. write:

> As local miners saw the growing economic disparity between the increasingly rich mine owners, the better paid miners in other parts of the state and themselves, tempers rose over both economic and civil rights issues. Not only did the miners demand to be paid more, but they wanted the freedom of speech and congregation to which they were entitled under the US Constitution (307).

A series of skirmishes across southern West Virginia led to the eventual Battle of Blair Mountain. In this battle, over 10,000 miners fought around 3,000 better-armed mercenaries. After the conflict, coal operators used federal and state-sponsored legal actions to destroy the coal miners' union and prosecute its leaders. For most of history, the event has been seen as a loss for organized labor, but recent recoveries have emphasized the watershed nature of Blair Mountain, as it captured powerful stories "about people no longer willing to be controlled, exploited, and violently abused from above" (Harris 91).

Especially significant were the coalitions that miners built across race and ethnicity. In Matewan, West Virginia, a hub for organizing activity, Black and white families lived near one another, a rare social dynamic for many American communities in the early 1900s. While company overseers tried to keep workers apart to prevent unionization, this strategy didn't work; one story to emerge in multiple primary sources documents Black and white miners holding cafeteria workers at gunpoint so that they would be served together, rather than separately, showing that they understood that they had to work together to improve their conditions (Hood, n.p.). This history challenges representations of Appalachia's workers as monolithically white and intolerant of others and illuminates the often-unrecognized role that workers from different backgrounds played in the state's history.

Despite its importance to state and national history, by many accounts, Blair Mountain is grossly overlooked. Shogan writes, "Among labor's many costly defeats, the Battle of Blair Mountain arguably ranks as the most neglected" due to our country's cultural attachment to the "middle-class ethos" (ix-x). However, in recent years, there have been efforts to recover Blair Mountain's importance—including by archival and educational organizations like the West Virginia Regional and History Center that have worked to preserve these under-recognized aspects of history.

Archival research in the writing classroom demonstrates the dynamic nature of archives where text, collaboration, and activism come together (Hayden and Graban), rather than simply serving as repositories of knowledge (Kirsch and Rohan). Broadly, Douglas describes archival research as a practice that "builds solidarity through reciprocal relationships around a central idea" (38). More specifically, others theorize the relationship between perceptions of place and archival research. Proszak and Cushman write that an archive is "both a repository grounded in place and a place of ever-shifting perspectives that continuously reorients its participants" (199), and archival projects allow students to "generate new knowledges about themselves and the places they reside in relation to history" (209).

Because archives present artifacts that interpreters then place into narratives, students must examine the relationship between those artifacts and the histories they know—or don't—and highlight the little narratives that often go unnoticed. Mastrangelo writes that archival projects require students to "grapple with the fact that local history has been reframed in ways that benefit the institution but are not necessarily respectful of or even directly connected" to marginalized figures (42). In our project, students examined their own interpretations of West Virginia, finding firsthand accounts of life in mining camps that challenged monolithic representations of the state and its people. Students found that the historical realities of West Virginia and its people are much more complex than any headline can capture, and in fact, offer a very different portrait of a place that one might initially expect—an outcome of increased place-based literacy.

Institutional Context

As outlined above, West Virginia is often represented in ways that are oversimplified (at best) and grossly stereotyped (at worst). The land grant institution at which I teach is deeply intertwined with these representations, making it a generative space for designing projects that address West Virginia as a whole. A project that addresses an underacknowledged element of the state's history, especially one that demonstrates how progressive its residents can be, is a powerful way to engage students in work that can shape their feelings towards the place in which they find themselves living–especially at a time when students constantly see their place ridiculed via popular narratives.

Multimedia Writing is an upper-level course taught within our department's English program. It enrolls upper-level students within a range of majors, including English, Journalism, Communications, Graphic Design, and Multidisciplinary Studies. While course projects vary according to instructor, as with many upper-level courses, the class is typically designed around writing and designing texts for online environments, usually culminating in a web design project.

During the semester that I taught this course synchronously online, there were students from branch campuses that were not located in the city in which I teach. This is unusual, since there are normally only synchronous in-person sections and asynchronous online sections; however, this COVID-era anomaly allowed for a more meaningful experience for all students. The presence of students from around the state contributed to the power of this project, as students collaborated across geographic distance to learn more about the state's often-hidden histories. Additionally, students at branch campuses are often nontraditional students who work full-time. Those students offer different perspectives on labor politics to more traditional college-aged students on our main campus, which enriched our classroom discussions and illuminated the importance of coalition-building across different groups—one of the key factors in the story of Blair Mountain.

In Spring 2021, I taught two sections of Multimedia Writing and collaborated with the West Virginia and Regional History Center's (WVRHC) Instruction and Public Services Archivist, Miriam Cady. The WVRHC was preparing to celebrate West Virginia Day, an annual celebration of state history and culture that marks the state's admission to the Union in 1863 after seceding from Virginia during the Civil War. Since 2021 marked the 100th anniversary of the Battle of Blair Mountain, the WVRHC wanted their programming to amplify their collections related to the Mine Wars. Part of the WVRHC's mission is to engage undergraduate and graduate students in their programming, oftentimes by introducing students to archival research. As a result, planning and executing this project involved more collaboration with Miriam than any other client-based project I had taken on before, resulting in a robust experience for students as they engaged with our partner throughout the semester, rather than just at the end.

I first met Miriam and learned more about the WVRHC while serving on a university-level committee planning a Wikipedia Edit-a-thon focused on amplifying stories about Appalachian artists and creators from marginalized groups in Fall 2020.

We worked together to plan an asynchronous event where students would be working with secondary research as well as digitized collections from the archives in their efforts to contribute to Wikipedia pages about underrepresented Appalachians. Over the course of working on this project, Miriam and I began to discuss possibilities for more direct collaboration between my courses and the WVRHC, specifically through a client-based project that would serve the needs of that organization while also providing students with a valuable experience. Miriam felt that there was significant value in tying the project into programming for the Blair Mountain anniversary, both in terms of sharing an often-overlooked aspect of West Virginia history with students and providing students with a clear exigency for their work.

She proposed that the final project in the course be a series of online exhibits built around holdings from the WVRHC's archives. Given Multimedia Writing's focus on designing digital texts for public audiences, these exhibits were an appropriate way to meet course goals. Because this promised to be a challenging project, due to the assignment's requirements that pushed students to learn about a historical event (in an English course, no less), to conduct secondary and archival research about that event, and to design online exhibits using a software platform that was entirely new for them, we knew that scaffolding the course at large would be key for any sort of success. Together, we developed a preliminary schedule, which included class visits from Miriam for instruction about archives and team meetings between her and students.

At the start of the semester, I began class with general principles of multimedia and digital writing, asking students to consider the rhetorical elements of texts that go viral. The second unit asked students to participate in the aforementioned Wikipedia Edit-a-thon sponsored by the university libraries, in which students contributed to pages about underrepresented Appalachian creators, including writers, poets, musicians, artists, and other creative minds. Then, students would take what they had learned about narrative and underrepresentation in digital spaces and apply that in the final project—the exhibits about Blair Mountain.

The final project itself was divided into smaller sections to both make the project feel more manageable for students and to allow myself and Miriam opportunities to check in with teams to ensure that they were on track to complete the project successfully. Miriam visited class several times to provide archival instruction and to teach us about the Battle itself. To get students started, Miriam and I brainstormed possible topics that students could use as initial steps for inquiry, and we used these topics to allow students to self-select into teams based on their interest and working style. Topics included organizing tactics, roles of women and children, union perspectives, and company histories. Several times throughout this last unit, usually in conjunction with a deliverable, we met with project teams (sometimes together and sometimes individually) to provide further guidance and support.

The assignment was divided into the smaller following sections:

- Digital Exhibit User Experience Analysis, a short assignment that asked students to look at examples of online exhibits to consider what elements they might want to incorporate in their own work;

- Exhibit Proposal, a general statement about the team's overall approach, strategy, and project planning;
- Exhibit Storyboard, a visual representation of what artifacts they planned to use and how pages would be organized;
- Reading & Research Log, an ongoing assignment that asked students to summarize and analyze sources they were finding about their topic;
- Digital Exhibit, the final deliverable, which displayed archival artifacts contextualized through secondary research and writing (created with Omeka, a platform often used by libraries and archives to display collections);
- Exhibit Rationale, a short document detailing the decisions teams made in creating their exhibit, which served as a sort of "read me" document for the WVRHC; and
- Postmortem Write-Up, a report that gave students the opportunity to reflect on the project and the teamwork they engaged in.

Because of the daunting nature of this project we felt that it was important to make the sections feel reasonable and achievable for students. Breaking the project into (many) steps gave us opportunities to engage with teams throughout the process and to troubleshoot any issues. Further, each smaller assignment helped to boost students' confidence as they learned more about their topics and increased their familiarity with archival research, digital design, and Blair Mountain as a whole.

One very important note before I move on: This was an ambitious project, and only possible because I had one prep that semester, since I was teaching two sections of the same course on my 2/2 teaching load. Because this project is so tied up with labor politics, I want to acknowledge my privilege in terms of being a tenure-track faculty member at a large research institution with much more institutional support than many of my peers. I point this out not only to encourage others in similar positions to take on these labor-intensive projects, but also to point to the structural elements that simultaneously enable some people to take these projects on while preventing others from doing the same. As advocated by the CCCC Statement on Community-Engaged Projects in Rhetoric and Composition, rich, in-depth, vibrant community-engaged teaching should be supported by institutional policies across ranks and positions—it should be a widely-accepted use of our time in the academy rather than an extraordinary feat or an outcome of an individual's privilege.

Student Outcomes

Students created 9 online exhibits dedicated to different topics related to the Battle of Blair Mountain; the exhibits can be viewed here: https://wvrhc.lib.wvu.edu/events/west-virginia-day/exhibits/2021/engl-303-student-exhibits. Each group had significant freedom in their approach, visible in the exhibits that offer multiple points of view and showcase a range of archival materials. While some groups chose to examine stakeholders who are often not included in stories that do circulate about Blair

Mountain, like women and children, others opted to focus on the experiences of miners themselves.

At the end of the semester, I asked students to complete a survey about the project, including aspects such as archival research, history content, client work, and digital storytelling (see Appendix). This survey was approved by my institution's IRB (#2104286435). The outcomes described in this section come from that survey, as well as reflective writing that students completed as part of the course. Twenty-seven out of forty-eight enrolled students responded to the survey. Any student names used are pseudonyms.

Students generally agreed that the project was useful in preparing them for work beyond college classrooms through its focus on learning new technologies, conducting research, and managing a client-based project. They also reported strengthening their information literacy skills due to their evaluation of primary texts as they conducted secondary research to better understand the contexts shaping those primary sources, and in their cataloging of archival sources on their pages using the appropriate metadata practices for the WVRHC. However, another finding emerged: students found themselves thinking *a lot* about place. Because archival collections are oftentimes organized around particular events, people, or places, holdings often point to place in significant ways. As students perused pictures, maps, newspaper articles, and other artifacts that referenced place in perhaps unanticipated ways, they began to understand different perspectives about West Virginia, some of which surprised them. Sixty five percent of student survey respondents said they had never done archival research before, but at the end of the project, most students stated that they were more comfortable with archival work. This is a significant outcome for a project that took place over roughly eight weeks, and, matched with the outcomes below, this result suggests that place-based archival projects offer a host of benefits for writing courses. Most importantly, such projects encourage students to find those little narratives that often go unheeded, which in can in turn reshape their own perceptions and communications about that place.

Outcome 1: Place-based archival projects complicated overarching, dominant narratives about place

Overall, most students stated that they had very little or no knowledge of the Battle of Blair Mountain. Only one student out of thirty-eight enrolled, a double major in English and History, reported more than a passing knowledge of the Mine Wars. Many of the students in these sections had attended high school in West Virginia or (obviously) had lived in West Virginia for several years as they attended college, resulting in both a more nuanced perception of the state and for many, frustration with stereotypical media narratives. Throughout these projects, students encountered primary artifacts and secondary research pointing towards a progressive history that challenged negative stereotypes. As a result, this project was transformative for us as a group, even if it was incredibly challenging to teach what was essentially a crash course in history even as we worked to develop exhibits in an English class.

When asked how much their knowledge of West Virginia history had changed because of this project, the twenty-seven survey respondents responded with a mean of 4.52 on a scale of 0-5 (with 0 being no change at all and 5 being a significant change). Several students noted that they had never even heard of the Battle of Blair Mountain before this project: their development over the course of the project was perhaps the most dramatic. Another common theme of responses was the respect that students had gained for working-class Appalachians who had challenged corporate interests and, by extension, one-dimensional stereotypes about the region. Macy, who grew up in West Virginia, wrote in her post-project reflection that she was "very passionate about how underrepresented West Virginia is in our media and society, so this project was a great way for me to show the WVRHC audience something about West Virginia's labor and mining culture, which is a huge part of West Virginia's culture in general."

One team focused specifically on media accounts of the Battle of Blair Mountain. In their research, this team combed databases and archival materials for articles from local, national, and even international newspapers. Among their findings was that the further away a newspaper was located from the conflict, the more sympathetic that account would be; more specifically, articles in local and state newspapers typically presented company interests as the righteous party, while national and international outlets suggested support for the miners with headlines such as, "Plot to hang miners' secretary in West Virginia halted but coal kings boast convictions of four" (*The Daily Worker,* Chicago, Illinois). They also discovered that when newspapers in West Virginia failed to fall in line with the company's narrative, those newspapers were often mysteriously shut down. This lack of local reporting resulted in "secrecy around the battle" (Hannah, post-project reflection). Drawing from their own surprise at this outcome, students felt it was important to emphasize this for their audience, who would presumably be made up of people interested in West Virginia and its history but perhaps not familiar with the complexities of Blair Mountain. This team chose to juxtapose the two divergent narratives perpetuated by different types of media outlets and to provide context for why those narratives were so wildly different, drawing connections to modern controversies that intertwine media and politics. In this way, students shared multiple little narratives that exhibit viewers could interpret themselves.

In their exhibit rationale, the media team wrote: "Our final exhibit brings attention to the many discrepancies that came with a battle fueled by greed on the part of coal company owners and desperation on the part of West Virginia coal miners. It is always important to inspect and critique media coverage of large events and the Battle of Blair Mountain is no exception." This team chose to emphasize how media sources are powerful actors in how places and people are perceived because of students' own realizations within the project. Their skepticism—and that of their classmates—toward reliable secondary sources heightened their valuing of primary archival research and fostered the development of a more critical view towards the powers that document a place's history and tell its stories.

Outcome 2: Place-based archival projects illuminated the presence of less visible stakeholders

Another significant outcome of our project was attention to new actors in the stories that shaped student perceptions of West Virginia. Students emerged from their work more familiar with people that they had not initially considered to be part of the story of the event, including women, children, and Black and immigrant coal miners. This new knowledge was reflected in their exhibits, as they chose to emphasize not just the presence of these groups but their contributions to the events, offering audience members little narratives of the state's history that have largely been lost.

Out of nine student teams, three teams chose to research the role of women or families in coal camps. Most groups mentioned Mother Jones, a labor activist not unknown to labor histories; however, because labor histories tend to focus on the struggles of male workers, especially in physically intensive jobs like coal mining, students were intrigued to learn that women (beyond Mother Jones) were significant contributors to labor struggles in Appalachia throughout the last century (see Wilkerson). As one student wrote in her post-project reflection, "The common narrative (though uncommon itself) about the Battle of Blair Mountain usually regards the histories of the male laborers and the men on the front lines of the battle. In our research, we discovered an entire other realm of participation in the battle from an at-home or female perspective that is very valuable" (Allison). This value, however, was not easily found for these teams as they ran into archival silences, or "[gaps] in the historical record resulting from the unintentional or purposeful absence or distortion of documentation" ("Archival Silences", n.p.).

Since women were not viewed as central to the struggles by most documentarians of the Mine Wars, primary artifacts like photographs and journal entries showing their involvement were not as readily available. As a result, students relied heavily on oral histories and brief newspaper accounts to illuminate the importance of women in this specific series of events. One artifact that appeared in multiple student exhibits was a newspaper article titled "Logan County bristles with machine guns," with the following opening line: "Its men, gaunt and hollow-eyed from long periods without sleep, are commanding the ridges. Its women and children have manned field kitchens back of the front while big army trucks are rushing food and ammunition to the defenders in the front line" (*The Washington Times*, Washington, D.C.). Teams that included this article pointed to the material necessity of women and children in providing food and support to the miners and allies involved in the conflict—a necessity that is not reflected in many primary or secondary accounts of the Mine Wars. This example demonstrated to students the value of multi-faceted research approaches that might bring into focus previously unnoticed actors due to archival silences.

In addition to gender, race and ethnicity were other identity factors that led students to unexpected findings throughout their research. As Smith argues, whiteness dominates representations of Appalachia, including West Virginia, and that whiteness shapes widespread perceptions of rural occupations like coal mining. As a result, many historical accounts emphasize the plight of poor white workers a group that has received a lot of attention in recent years in popular narratives about Appalachia discussed earlier in this piece. Students working on this project, however, read prima-ry accounts from miners that had recently immigrated from Eastern Europe and Italy as well as Black miners originally from the Deep South, complicating their percep-tions of who might have been a coal miner in the 1920s.

One team that focused specifically on miners' organizing activities leading up to the Battle wrote in their exhibit rationale that to exclude background information about how the miners built connections across identity groups "risks boiling the Bat-tle down to nothing more than a spontaneous fight involving men and rifles, when in reality, it was a conflict that consisted of years of struggle, and included high levels of organization and cooperation between different races, genders, and classes of people." That same group showcased photographs that showed Black and white miners pos-ing together, as well as the lyrics to a song entitled "Solidarity Forever." This song was sung to the tune of "John Brown's Body," a song about abolitionist John Brown who incited a rebellion of enslaved people at Harper's Ferry, West Virginia in 1859. In-cluding these specific artifacts that tie the Battle of Blair Mountain to larger historical narratives more well-known to exhibit audiences is a particular strategy that several student groups took on: assembling little stories and connecting them to cultural nar-ratives through juxtaposition or refutation was a common approach across exhibits. Students made these choices, I believe, to foster the same surprise in audiences that they themselves had experienced after learning more about the diversity of coal towns in the early 20th century and to suggest that this historical event could offer a model for coalition-building today.

Outcome 3: Place-based archival projects invited deeper understanding of latent identity factors such as socioeconomic class

Because Blair Mountain is explicitly categorized as a labor uprising, socioeconomic class was an important concept from the start of this project; however, it soon became clear that many students were not initially familiar or even comfortable with conver-sations about class. Over the course of the project each team addressed class in some way in their exhibits, revealing a more nuanced understanding of how socioeconomic inequality shaped events related to Blair Mountain and ultimately served as a basis for coalition-building across multiple identity groups. Throughout their projects, stu-dents considered how dominant narratives tend to collapse different identities and in turn, sought out narratives that illuminate how identity shapes experience.

Part of this focus on socioeconomic class might be due to the readings we com-pleted as a group, as many texts highlighted the role of class consciousness in building movements. A particular favorite among students was Abby Lee Hood's piece "The Battle of Blair Mountain was the largest labor uprising in U.S. History," part of *Teen Vogue*'s OG History series. Additionally, archival materials referenced the importance of class identity consistently. Many newspaper articles described the miners as "poor" or as "workers" and many physical materials were tied to class as well. Students were intrigued by the WVRHC's collection of scrip, or company-issued currency that min-ers could only redeem in company-owned stores. Students working on the "Life in

Company Towns" exhibit provided pictures of scrip and company stores juxtaposed with excerpts from oral histories from miners explaining how everything they bought was from a company store, at company-set prices. The team wrote on their page titled "Economic Control":

> Miners and their families were forced to be entirely dependent on coal companies. Living in company-owned housing and being paid in company-specific currency prevented many from being able to quit their jobs or move to another town (Wagner, 2011). They were forced to stay in the company town, where coal operators could continue making a profit.

This model, vastly different from the world-wide commerce that students today experience, illuminated the material impacts of class-based struggle. Students' framing of the model directly challenges romantic narratives about hardworking coal miners and benevolent companies—narratives that continue to circulate today.

For many students, the exploitation that miners faced demonstrated the links between place and class. One student wrote in their final reflection, "We knew that the miners were being taken advantage of from the mining companies, but we didn't know to what extent. We felt that we needed to give our audience a feel of how big and impactful this event was to West Virginia" (Cassidy). Echoing this sentiment, another student wrote in their survey response that they "gained a lot of respect for working-class Appalachia and got a better understanding of how the state got to where it is now." Instead of relying on simplistic narratives about West Virginia and surrounding areas that have a rich history of coal mining—a history that glorifies coal mining and other manual occupations—students gained a more critical understanding of that history. They emerged from the project with a deeper understanding of how corporate forces have historically disenfranchised the working class, troubling one-dimensional narratives that glorify capitalism and ignore corporate exploitation.

Outcome 4: Place-based archival projects encouraged students to contextualize relationships between artifacts, research, and their own histories

Providing students with the opportunity to wade through archival sources documenting events that took place near them offered new perspectives on their own connections to the project's subject matter. In this way, archival research helped students to position themselves in larger cultural narratives, including those that challenged dominant stereotypes. Repeatedly, students commented on their lack of familiarity with archival research and how they were learning to put archival materials into conversation with other sources, which was a different form of analysis than most had previously encountered.

As noted earlier, students ran into a number of archival silences that forced them to reconsider their plans as they developed their exhibits; but even as they found themselves wishing for certain artifacts that they couldn't access or that hadn't even been preserved, they embraced the challenge of contextualizing those materials via secondary research. As they sought to better understand the significance of the artifacts they *did* have access to, they found greater value in secondary accounts of the Battle as well. One survey respondent commented on the "wealth of artifacts out there that, while still remaining preserved, are beneficial to no one because they are not discovered and placed into the context of a narrative." Another student echoed this sentiment, saying that alone, the artifacts didn't initially mean much, "but after careful research I began to discover a lot of information." The storytelling lens of the project helped students to consider the relationships between different artifacts as they tried to create cohesive narratives that would guide audience members through their exhibits.

For several students, including many who had been born and raised in West Virginia, this project offered them the opportunity to reflect on their own identities and experiences and even to "revise" their sense of place, to use Carlo's words. Many students, either in their post-project reflections or in their survey responses, commented on how much they learned about West Virginia throughout the project. One response read, "It taught me a ton more information about my ancestors and relatives than I would have ever learned," signifying that students were thinking about their own personal connections to the events surrounding Blair Mountain. At the start of the project, one student asked if she could contribute primary sources to the WVRHC's archival collections, since her family possessed letters from her great grandfather (who was a child during the Mine Wars) talking about what he remembered from that period.

Some students shared very specific details in their feedback that referenced their own histories. One survey response read:

> I come from a small town in WV that was right by a lumber town (Lumberport, WV). There are also old coal mines boarded up randomly all over. Many of the places are on people's farm properties and they call them "the old mines"…I live within 15 minutes of an actual mine and can drive under the coal moving belts that extend across the roads. My grandfather also worked in the mines in and around my hometown.

Though this student's family history didn't necessarily connect with the Battle of Blair Mountain itself, their project had encouraged them to consider the connections between their familial histories and the photographs and other artifacts they were working with, finding parallels between what they were learning about and their own identities. Another student learned that their family lived on land associated with the Battle: "In fact, my Grandma currently lives on the Lens Creek Mountain, which I learned was part of the geography involved in the Battle of Blair Mountain. I have always loved West Virginia but learning about the richness of the history here always makes me love it more." This project urged students to learn more about not only the state's history, but their own, as well. They were able to identify little narratives—those in their own familiar histories as well as those hidden in the archives—and put them into conversation with larger, more dominant cultural narratives in ways that required exhibit audiences to reassess their own knowledge about labor histories.

Conclusion

This project was a huge undertaking that resulted in an incredibly valuable shared experience as students, myself, and the WVRHC worked toward a more nuanced understanding of West Virginia and its rich history—together. Our place-based archival project urged students to consider the importance of ethical storytelling as they sorted through primary artifacts in their quest to assemble accurate, nuanced narratives about the Battle of Blair Mountain and its legacy on labor history in West Virginia and beyond. Throughout the project, students reconsidered previously held notions about the state and reimagined their own connections to West Virginia and its history. They sought out little narratives that challenged dominant stories, laying them out beside one another and even weaving them together; they revised their sense of place as they recovered stories that presented a very different image of West Virginia than they were used to seeing and reimagined their own relationships to the state and its stories.

Many students originally from West Virginia commented on the fact that they had not been taught much about this labor history in primary or secondary school. Several student survey responses stated that while they knew that the coal mining industry had shaped the state's history, they did not know details of that history including "the poor conditions created by the coal mining industry." Some student responses stated explicitly that they had not previously received any instruction on these topics: "This project taught me a lot about the history of my state where high school education classes did not succeed in doing so" and "The amount of history and information that is archived shows to me how much rich history we have that isn't taught in schools." Interestingly, the comparison between what we discussed in class and their educational experiences in high school was a common refrain, presumably because of units that focused on West Virginia history in West Virginia high schools—albeit a sanitized, simplified version of the state's history.

Though it was not initially a stated outcome of this project, students' critical literacies—or awareness of the sociopolitical systems through which we live our lives and subsequent questioning of those systems (Vasquez, Janks, and Comber)—seemed to develop as well. As they read firsthand accounts of the Battle and examined newspaper articles detailing the ways that coal companies exploited miners and their families, students began to question their previously held beliefs about West Virginia and the region. For example, many West Virginians have connections to coal mining through family members or because of where they grew up, resulting in a shared sense of pride for coal communities. The coal industry has capitalized on that pride, framing it as pride for the industry as a whole—despite the realities of exploitation embedded in the industry's history. Two teams connected the historical events we learned about to the 2016 teacher's strikes in the state, noting the continued importance of collective action in the face of institutional power—especially in areas that are largely defined through one-dimensional narratives. Place-based archival projects are one method that writing instructors might consider in helping students to develop these literacy skills.

This increase in critical literacy resulted in not only a more nuanced understanding, but a greater sense of connection to place. Nearly every student who responded to the survey expressed feeling a greater emotional investment in West Virginia because of the project. One student wrote:

> It taught me so much, actually. I was a little shocked by how much I learned. It was so personally impactful too because I feel now that I am more proud of this silent past of our state more than anything I've read in the history books. It's also tremendously upsetting to me that most West Virginians know nothing about this truth.

While our client-based project could very easily have remained a project students completed in a classroom to practice skills they would need in their eventual careers, it seems to have had a deeper impact. Student work and responses suggested not only a re-imagination of their sense of connection to West Virginia, but a desire to educate others about the history—especially people in the state that have been affected by negative stereotypes, demonstrating an increased awareness of the material impacts that stories can have on communities.

By delving more deeply into a particular event with connections to local, state, and even national history, students honed their place-based literacy and related skills as they thought critically about the ways that storytelling shapes a place and its people. By recovering the stories of Blair Mountain, students reconsidered their own feelings towards the state and narratives that they had heard, revising their senses of place. Providing opportunities for students to sit with place through research and writing while simultaneously drawing on student knowledge about our shared places can be a transformative classroom experience. Ultimately, place matters—especially as we seek to build coalitions across our communities that embrace values of justice, equality, and care.

Acknowledgments

I would like to thank Miriam Cady at the West Virginia and Regional History Center for her massive support of this project, and the students who took on the complicated and rewarding work of place-based archival research and digital storytelling.

Appendix

ENGL 303 Digital Storytelling Study Survey

Start of Block: Default Question Block

Q1 You are invited to participate in this research study related to the digital storytelling project in ENGL 303. The following information is provided in order to help you to make an informed decision whether or not to participate. If you have any questions, please do not hesitate to ask.

You are eligible to participate because you are at least 18 years old and you are enrolled in a section of ENGL 303 in Spring 2021. Again, you must be 18 years old to be eligible for this study.

The purpose of this study is to better understand how digital storytelling projects can help students meet learning outcomes in multimedia writing. If you agree to participate, you will complete a brief survey. The information gained from this study may help us better understand how projects like this can serve as sites of learning.

Participation in this study will require approximately 5-10 minutes of your time. Your response will be anonymous, as your name will not be collected. All data will be held in confidence by the researcher in a secure file. Your participation in this study is voluntary. You are free to decide not to participate in this study without adversely affecting your relationship with the investigators or the institution.

Once you have started the survey, even after you consent to participate, you may withdraw from the study by exiting the survey if you decide you no longer wish to participate. However, once you submit your survey, you cannot withdraw, as your responses are anonymous, and so the researcher would not be able to identify and delete your response. Your decision to respond to the survey or not will not result in any loss of benefits to which you are otherwise entitled.

Potential benefits of your participation may include a more thoughtful realization about learning outcomes and participatory experience related to digital storytelling and client projects. The risks associated with participating in this study are no greater than those experienced in everyday life.

If you are willing to participate in this study, please click "yes." Saying yes will take you to the first survey question.

Primary Investigator:
[Removed for peer review]

This project has been approved by the [institution's] Institutional Review Board.

○ Yes, I consent to participate in this survey.

○ No, I do not consent to participate in this survey.

Q2 Did this project help you meet the following objectives of the course? (Check all that apply.)

☐ Discuss key elements of multimedia writing, including document design, user experience, interface and platform politics, and distribution/circulation

☐ Articulate connections between different types of multimedia and different elements of their past and current uses

☐ Reflect thoughtfully on the ethical questions that living in a networked, digital world invites (i.e. intellectual property, credibility, aggression in online spaces, etc.)

☐ Create effective documents in a range of multimedia formats and on a variety of platforms

☐ Manage research and analysis-focused projects in order to produce projects ready for public circulation, individually and collaboratively

Q3 Have you done team/collaborative projects before?

○ Yes

○ No

Display This Question:

If Have you done team/collaborative projects before? = Yes

Q3A How was this project similar or different?

_____

Q4 Have you done remote projects before?

○ Yes

○ No

Display This Question:

If Have you done remote projects before? = Yes

Q4A How was this project similar or different?

_____

Q5 Have you done client-based projects before?

◯ Yes

◯ No

Display This Question:
If Have you done client-based projects before? = Yes

Q5A How was this project similar or different?

_____

Q6 Have you done archival research before?

◯ Yes

◯ No

Display This Question:
If Have you done archival research before? = Yes

Q6A How was this project similar or different?

_____

Q7 Please indicate how you feel that your skills or knowledges in the areas noted below have changed as a result of this project, with 0 being no change at all and 5 being a significant amount of development.

	0	1	2	3	4	5

Project management

Working remotely

Working collaboratively/in team situations

Archival research (finding and analyzing primary sources)

Academic research (finding and analyzing secondary sources)

Learning new technological platforms

Designing multimodal texts

Writing for public audiences

Digital storytelling

West Virginia history and culture

Q8 Are there other skills or knowledges that you feel you have developed as a part of this project? If so, please note those below.

_____

Q9 Do you think other client-based projects, similar to this one, would be useful to implement in other Professional Writing and Editing courses?

○ Extremely useful

○ Very useful

○ Moderately useful

○ Slightly useful

○ Not at all useful

Q10 Please elaborate on your answer above.

_____

Q11 Is there anything else you would like to share about your experience with this project?

_____

Works Cited

Alexander, Kara Poe. "Successes, Victims, and Prodigies: 'Master' and 'Little' Cultural Narratives in the Literacy Narrative Genre." *College Composition and Communication*, vol. 62, no. 4, 2011, pp. 608–33.

"Archival Silence." *Dictionary of Archives Terminology*, https://dictionary.archivists.org/entry/archival-silence.html. Accessed 30 Sept. 2022.

Carlo, Rosanne. "Keyword Essay: Place-Based Literacies." *Community Literacy Journal*, vol. 10, no. 2, 2016, pp. 59-70.

"CCCC Statement on Community-Engaged Projects in Rhetoric and Composition." https://cccc.ncte.org/cccc/resources/positions/community-engaged. Accessed 15 May 2023.

Donehower, Kim, Charlotte Hogg, and Eileen E. Schell. "Introduction." *Reclaiming the Rural: Essays on Literacy, Rhetoric, and Pedagogy*, edited by Kim Donehower, Charlotte Hogg, and Eileen E. Schell, SIU Press, 2012, pp. 1-13.

Douglas, Whitney. "Looking Outward: Archival Research as Community Engagement." *Community Literacy Journal*, vol. 11, no. 2, 2017, pp. 30-42.

Fagerjord, Anders. "Toward a Rhetoric of the Place: Creating Locative Experiences." *Rhetoric and Experience Architecture*, edited by Liza Potts & Michael J. Salvo, Parlor Press, 2017, pp. 225–240.

Flower, Linda. *Community Literacy and the Rhetoric of Public Engagement.* SIU Press, 2008.

Gruenewald, David A. "The Best of Both Worlds: A Critical Pedagogy of Place." *Educational Researcher*, vol. 32, no. 4, 2003, pp. 3-12.

Harris, Wess. "What if We Really Won the Battle of Blair Mountain?" *Appalachian Heritage*, vol. 39, no. 3, 2011, pp. 87-91.

Hayden, Wendy, and Tarez Samra Graban. "A Critical Introduction: Teaching Rhetoric and Composition through the Archives." *Teaching through the Archives: Text, Collaboration, and Activism*, edited by Wendy Hayden and Tarez Samra Graban, Southern Illinois University Press, 2022, pp. 1-30.

Hayes, Amanda. "Place, Pedagogy, and Literacy in Appalachia." *English Education*, vol. 50, no. 1, 2017, pp. 72-89.

Herndl, Carl. G, Sarah Beth Hopton, Lauren Cutlip, Elena Yu Polush, Rick Cruse, and Mack Shelley. "What's a Farm? The Languages of Space and Place." *Field Rhetoric: Ethnography, Ecology, and Engagement in the Places of Persuasion.* University of Alabama Press, 2018, pp. 61-94.

Hood, Abby Lee. "What Made the Battle of Blair Mountain the Largest Labor Uprising in American History." *Smithsonian Magazine*, 25 Aug. 2021, https://www.smithsonianmag.com/history/battle-blair-mountain-largest-labor-uprising-american-history-180978520/. Accessed 8 Oct. 2022.

Humphreys, John H., Jane W. Gibson, and Jennifer D. Oyler. "Upward Defiance in Organizations: Management Lessons from the Battle of Blair Mountain." *Journal of Management History*, vol. 19, no. 3, 2013, pp. 304-327.

Kirsch, Gesa E., and Liz Rohan. "Introduction: The Role of Serendipity, Family Connections, and Cultural Memory in Historical Research." *Beyond the Archives: Re-*

search as a Lived Process, edited by Gesa E. Kirsch and Liz Rohan, Southern Illinois University Press, 2008, pp. 1-12.

Kurlinkus, Will, and Krista Kurlinkus. "Coal Keeps the Lights On." *College English*, vol. 81, no. 2, 2018, pp. 87-109.

Long, Elenore. *Community Literacy and the Rhetoric of Local Publics*. Parlor Press LLC, 2008.

Lyotard, Jean-Francois. *The Postmodern Condition: A Report on Knowledge*. Trans, by Geoff Bennington and Brian Massumi. Minneapolis: U of Minnesota P, 1999.

Martinez, Aja Y. "A Plea for Critical Race Theory Counterstory: Stock Story versus Counterstory Dialogues Concerning Alejandra's 'Fit' in the Academy." *Composition Studies*, vol. 42, no. 2, 2014, pp. 33–55.

Mastrangelo, Lisa. "Using the Archives to Teach Slow Research and Create Local Connections." *Teaching through the Archives: Text, Collaboration, and Activism*, edited by Wendy Hayden and Tarez Samra Graban, Southern Illinois University Press, 2022, pp. 31-45.

McNely, Brian. "Instagram, Geocaching, and the When of Rhetorical Literacies." *Kairos*, vol. 19, no. 3, 2015, https://kairos.technorhetoric.net/19.3/index.html. Accessed 19 Nov. 2022.

Plein, Stewart. "Portraits of Appalachia: The Identification of Stereotype in Publishers' Bookbindings, 1850-1915." *Journal of Appalachian Studies*, vol. 15, no. 1/2, 2009, pp. 99-115.

"Plot to hang miners' secretary in West Virginia halted but coal kings boast convictions of four." *The Daily Worker* [Chicago], 14 April, 1924, p. 3. *Chronicling America*, https://chroniclingamerica.loc.gov/lccn/sn84020097/1924-04-14/ed-1/seq-3/

Proszak, Laura, and Ellen Cushman. "Delinking Student Perceptions of Place with/in the University Archive." *Teaching through the Archives: Text, Collaboration, and Activism*, edited by Wendy Hayden and Tarez Samra Graban, Southern Illinois University Press, 2022, pp. 197-211.

Reynolds, Nedra. *Geographies of Writing: Inhabiting Places and Encountering Difference*, Southern Illinois University Press, 2004.

Rivers, Nathaniel A. "Geocomposition in Public Rhetoric and Writing Pedagogy." *College Composition and Communication*, vol. 67, no. 4, 2016, pp. 576-606.

Shogan, Robert. *The Battle of Blair Mountain: The Story of America's Largest Labor Uprising*. Basic Books, 2006.

Smith, Barbara Ellen. "De-gradations of whiteness: Appalachia and the complexities of race." *Journal of Appalachian Studies*, vol. 10, no. 1/2, 2004, pp. 38-57.

Vasquez, Vivian Maria, Hilary Janks, and Barbara Comer. "Key Aspects of Critical Literacy: An Excerpt." NCTE Blog. https://ncte.org/blog/2019/07/critical-literacy/. Accessed 18 May, 2023.

Webb-Sunderhaus, Sara, and Kim Donehower, eds. "Introduction." *Rereading Appalachia: Literacy, Place, and Cultural Resistance,* Southern Illinois University Press, 2004.

Webb-Sunderhaus, Sara. "'Keep the Appalachian, Drop the Redneck': Tellable Student Narratives of Appalachian Identity." *College English*, vol. 79, no. 1, 2016, pp. 11-33.

Weisser, Christian R., and Sidney I. Dobrin, eds. *Ecocomposition: Theoretical and Pedagogical Approaches.* SUNY Press, 2012.

Wilkerson, Jessica. *To Live Here, You Have to Fight: How Women Led Appalachian Movements for Social Justice.* University of Illinois Press, 2018.

Author Bio

Erin Brock Carlson is an assistant professor in the Department of English at West Virginia University, where she teaches undergraduate and graduate courses in Writing Studies. Her current research uses participatory approaches to study the relationships between place, technology, and community, specifically in rural areas.

Project and Program Profiles

Capacitating Community: The Writing Innovation Symposium

Jenn Fishman with Abigayle Farrier, Aleisha R. Balestri, Barbara Clauer, Bump Halbritter, Darci Thoune, Derek G. Handley, Gitte Frandsen, Holly Burgess, Lillian Campbell, Liz Angeli, Louise Zamparutti, Jenna Green, Jennifer Kontny, Jessica R. Edwards, Jessie Wirkus Haynes, Julie Lindquist, Kaia L. Simon, Kayla Urban Fettig, Kelsey Otero, Margaret Perrow, Maria Novotny, Marie Cleary-Fishman, Maxwell Gray, Melissa Kaplan, Patrick W. Thomas, Paul Feigenbaum, Sara Heaser, and Seán McCarthy

Abstract

The topic of this symposium, capacitating community, invites *CLJ* readers to consider what makes community possible. This piece showcases one means, small conferences, via a retrospective on the Writing Innovation Symposium (WIS), a regional event with national scope that has hosted writers and writing educators annually in Milwaukee, WI, since 2018. Through a quilted conversation pieced from hours of small-group discussion, twenty-nine participants across academic and nonacademic ranks, roles, and ranges of experience offer insight into the WIS as well as the nature and value of professional community.

Keywords: capacity building, community, conference, innovation, professional community, symposium, writing, writing education

Introduction

Jenn Fishman

The Writing Innovation Symposium (WIS) is a regional meeting with national reach that welcomes participants annually to balmy, mid-winter Milwaukee, Wisconsin. My role is Chief Capacitator. It's a nonce title given to me by Seán McCarthy, and its story is signature WIS. The occasion was a manuscript workshop that featured an article-in-progress by Seán and Paul Feigenbaum. Like other WIS programming, including plenary presentations, five-minute flashtalks,[1] and research displays, the workshop was, above all, an occasion for co-work. That day, our small but representative group included not only faculty and graduate students but also a university arts outreach coordinator, Melissa Kaplan, and a hospital association administrator, Marie Cleary-Fishman. Then, as always, we discussed, and we engaged one another through discussion. We wrote independently and together. We ate—and ate well—and it happened: there was synergy and serendipity, invention and innovation, and among so many other things, Seán put words to the role I play as steward of it all.

The WIS itself rose phoenix-like from the ashes of my university's writing program, which was eliminated while the symposium was in planning stages. From the start, Marquette University's Social Innovation Initiative anchored the WIS, and the University Libraries provided the primary location. The writing program, First-Year English, was to be the compass, guiding whatever directions the symposium might take. I was WPA at the time, and I co-founded WIS with the program's graduate assistant director, Jessie Wirkus Haynes; Kelsey Otero, then Director for Innovation at Marquette's 707 Hub; and Elizabeth Gibes, then Marquette's digital scholarship librarian. Despite uncertain times, we persisted, inviting plenary presentations about the persistence of writers and writing, and now I helm the cross-institutional steering committee that formed on the heels of the first symposium in 2018.

Typically, the WIS takes place in the third week of Marquette's spring semester. Our second year, we withstood a polar vortex; the following year, 2020, the WIS was the last in-person conference that many of us attended until we resumed in 2022, masks and vaxes required. In 2023, our sophomore year as a hybrid event and our fifth anniversary, we gathered under the umbrella of "Writing As _____." Previous themes include "Connect!," "Just Writing," and "Write It Out," all phrases that signal our commitment to exploring the deeply human activity of writing as not only praxes and products but also lived experiences, relations, and related ethical considerations. Although we initially imagined the WIS as a local, "drivable" event, we circulated the CFP widely, and our first proposal was from colleagues in New Jersey. Each year, we have registered approximately 100 people from across ranks and roles within and beyond higher education. To date, although many participants come from Wisconsin, WIS has involved writers and writing educators from 22 states and provinces.

In writing studies, small conferences have big presence, including regional affiliate events supported by national professional organizations and events coordinated by one or more host campuses, programs, and endowments. The WIS is a cross-institutional enterprise based (so far) at a single university (Marquette), funded mainly through registration ($25-$100 for onsite; $15-$60 for online). Regular support (e.g., space, stewardship) comes from Marquette's Social Innovation Initiative, Libraries, and Haggerty Museum of Art, while funding for plenary speakers and special features has come from Marquette's Center for Teaching and Learning and Office of Community Engagement, plus Mount Mary University. Additionally, Bedford/St. Martin's has made possible a fellows program, which offers selected participants (including contributors Holly Burgess and Abigayle Farrier) funding, mentorship, and an opportunity to contribute to the *Bedford Bits* blog.

Over five years, WIS has done more than foster professional community among colleagues with shared interest in writing. WIS has also become a community, which the quilted conversation below represents. Each section is culled from recorded conversations organized around prompts that asked contributors to reflect on what drew them to WIS, their experience(s), and their takeaways. Certainly, there is magic in what we do together; the WIS is also the result of an always-evolving collaborative design, which is well-reflected in this twenty-nine-person retrospective. However, readers most interested in the "how to" are welcome to skip right to the recipe at the end.

On behalf of all WISe ones, symposers past and future, I invite you to join us.

Such a Cool Little Thing

*Darci Thoune, Jennifer Kontny, Patrick Thomas, and Sara Heaser are long-time members of the WIS Steering Committee. As core organizers, they have also led efforts to develop symposium themes, establish the Bedford/St. Martin's Fellows (Darci), and select and mentor plenary presenters (Jennifer and Patrick).

Darci: I remember Sara was sitting in my office, and we saw the first CFP. Just the word innovation got us. It was like, yeah, we need to be talking about innovation.

Sara: I was also drawn to the word innovation, and I thought that first CFP talked about writing in a really authentic way, as a tool that all people use. I distinctly remember the call for librarians, scientists, teachers, writers, community workers, people from all areas of the community to come together and talk about writing. And I think that's what got me excited.

Darci: I remember that first CFP, that invitation to collaborate, to play, to reimagine, and we continue to do that every year. It could be so easy to sort of slip into, "Well, this worked last year. Let's just do it this way next year." But we resist that, and it's by design. And so WIS continues to be invitational or seeks to invite and innovate in new ways every year.

Sara: We're also not tied to one idea of what WIS has to be. I actually think that we are most tied to honoring what writing is, who it serves, and in what capacity. This year we opened up with two hours of writing time. To me that was radical, because writing itself often gets pushed off, right? It's often the last thing we give ourselves time to do, but it's actually the most important thing. And to devote time like that, to sit in a room of writers writing together, I think that really speaks to the spirit of what WIS is.

Patrick: I have come to think of each WIS as really a respite and a place of shared reflection about what we're doing and why it might be important. It's not only having the kind of social and intellectual space to share ideas but also being able to have the aspects of the gathering that are less formal, less scheduled: taking time with present-ers or with other participants, having immediate reflection and response.

Sara: As steering committee members, we very purposefully think about what kind of experience people are going to have. It's not about content, in a way. And I like how you said, Patrick, that you see this as a respite. I love that you use that word because I think that's our intention. We want people to come and really have the shared reflec-tive experience of thinking about writing.

Darci: The WIS is always social by design. Like you spend the whole day there in the basement of Raynor Libraries, and we just kind of hunker down together. Those are really precious moments.

Jennifer: I think of WIS as an invitation to give sustained energy and intellectual at-tention—but also social attention—to people who are positioned in really different ways across institutions in their relationship to writing in general and in their trajec-tory as writers and people who are invested in writing as a profession or professional-ly, I should say.

Darci: Another one of the things I really like about the way we design WIS is that it's incredibly affordable. We make it so that people who may not get much funding can come. And there's a certain lack of pretension that goes with the invitational nature of the CFP every year—although I certainly do get star struck. I mean, like, we always have luminaries that come every year, and it feels very good to be able to talk to these people that you admire in this low pressure, lowkey, we're-having-a-glass-of-wine-looking-at-a-poster-session kind of way.

Patrick: I think part of what makes it not just invitational but also an invitation that people accept is it's a different kind of academic gathering that emphasizes people's strengths over sharing work for more critical review. The latter certainly happens, but it doesn't happen through the same mechanisms of critique as other conferences. It happens through a more open, non-hierarchical, and looser set of interests than what can often feel like gatekeeping or insider/outsider kinds of dynamics, where it's like, you know, God forbid, if you don't know the secret handshake. That's just not part of our agenda. It's more, to Jennifer's earlier point, like we take writing seriously but across the real, full range of what writing can be.

Jennifer: I feel like most conference presentations, whether they be roundtables or panels, are like mini-exhibitions of sorts, where the message is pre-crafted, and you're supposed to take something away. But I feel like what we're doing is more akin to cre-ating rooms that are like installations, and they're not locked into the timeframe of a panel or workshop, and their meaning evolves.

Darci: There's something about the WISes that are rather magical, like things are going to happen every year, something is going to happen, and I'm going to be taking it away with me.

Jennifer: Such a cool little thing we've built together.

Q&A

WIS attendees Abigayle Farrier, Derek Handley, Gitte Frandsen, Holly Burgess, Kaia Simon, Louise Zamparutti, and Margaret Perrow reflect on their experiences.

Question: What drew you initially to the Writing Innovation Symposium?

Kaia: So, it was my first year out of graduate school, and Jenn sent an email to several people in the region. I chose to attend because I was looking for community. I was hoping also to learn more about how to direct a writing program because I was doing that from the get-go and really looking to connect with folks who could help and mentor me.

Derek: I think I first heard of the WIS from my colleague Shavon Watson, but I started at UWM during the pandemic, and nothing was really going on. I really didn't start paying attention to WIS until I received the email invitation from Patrick Thomas about possibly being a speaker—and I, of course, jumped on the opportunity. I was really interested in Jessica Edwards' workshop that year, and I wanted to bring my class this past year because I had been so pleasantly surprised. It wasn't just a regional conference.

Gitte: So, the first time I attended was in 2020, when I was a first-year PhD student, and an advanced PhD student, Molly Ubbusen, invited me to join a panel. I was super excited. I was terrified. It was the first time I've ever attended a conference and given a talk. Then, this year I was excited to join again because I had been working with a fellow Graduate Teaching Assistant mom about what it means to be in grad school as a first-gen student and a mom of younger children. When we saw the call for "Writing As _____," it felt like a really perfect call for us.

Louise: I think I was drawn to WIS initially because I knew people who were part of the organizational team, including some of my colleagues at UW-La Crosse. And WIS 2022 was the first in-person conference for me since the pandemic, and I was very eager to see people in person. But mostly I wanted to share my work and receive feedback.

Holly: I received my master's degree from Marquette and am currently in the PhD program; however, I had never heard of the WIS. Two of my colleagues mentioned that they were presenting at the WIS this year. I attended the WIS as I thought the poster session would be a great way to show my dissertation visually. Creating the poster allowed me to map out my dissertation and present my work.

Abigayle: The fall of 2021 was the first time I taught a composition course at the university level. I'm a literature PhD student, and all my literature friends had told me composition is just something you have to get through. But then I loved comp! I enjoyed it so much that a professor suggested I look into some comp conferences, and so I found WIS.

Margaret: I found out about it from a colleague who'd received an email. She sent it to me and said, "This sounds like it's right up your alley." I looked at it and thought, 'Oh, no, not one more thing to do.' But something just flipped a switch. I was like, 'I am so exhausted and overwhelmed. I need some fun. And, yes, this looks like the perfect place to share the work that I've been doing with my students.'

Question: What were the highlights of your WIS experience(s)?

Louise: In 2022 it was just great to be back at an in-person conference, and it was also my first conference as a faculty member (rather than a graduate student). By participating in WIS, I felt so much less alone. Then, in 2023 I loved the format of the flashtalk. It made me really condense my presentation, which was about assaultive speech in relation to monuments that I study and some really quite violent examples of graffiti on campus. I gave a flashtalk about that and got great feedback.

Gitte: The concurrent session that my colleague and I presented at this year was called "Bodies of Work." It featured other grad students who spoke about composing in the pool, writing as being, and writing assistance. The format of five-minute flashtalks really made everyone stay super focused, and we had a lot of time for talk at the end that was just so full of energy and synergy. Even the people who livestreamed felt like they were in the room.

Derek: I enjoyed the panels that I heard this year. They were mostly graduate students presenting on writing when you're not actually writing—one man was talking about when he is swimming laps when he's composing—and then a couple of graduate students shared their experiences of what it's like to be parents and in grad school and on the job market. Listening to all those things is helpful for me when mentoring and advising graduate students.

Holly: I had a lot of fun. Hearing what other people were working on was interesting. I liked the poster session I was a part of. I thought having it during the reception was a great idea because it was low stakes. People were moving around and mingling. I received great feedback on my dissertation, with attendees pointing out things I hadn't considered. It's great when people approach you and say, "Hey, did you notice this link in your work?" and "That resonated with me."

Margaret: The project that I proposed was a presentation, but what came back quickly from Jenn and Max was an invitation to do an interactive website instead. I thought that sounded like a really cool challenge, and I'm happy to report that it turned out great. It was really fun to make; it was really fun to share; and the venue, which was the reception, was fantastic. I liked the conversations that happened when people came to the table and watched the student videos. Also, being able to give my students feedback from WIS attendees was really powerful. That presentation format is something that I would like to emulate at Southern Oregon University.

Abigayle: One of the things that stood out to me was the dinner the night before the symposium began. It was really wonderful to meet everyone. They were all so kind to take three grad students from Texas out to dinner and introduce themselves before everything really got kicked off. And then during the symposium, there was one panel just for grad students. It was great to be able to have that space to just talk with other graduate students, especially ones who were not from my own university.

Kaia: One of the things that stands out to me about the WISes I attended was the extent to which I felt like I was being hosted. I remember feeling truly like a guest, like I had been invited and that my presence mattered. Another thing about the overall experience was that it really was about writing. Each year there was a session where we were writing: we were creative writing, and we were writing collaboratively. I also think it's one of the only conferences I've been to where the conversations continue. Part of that is because you can get your arms around WIS, you know, like we're all kind of together. I really appreciate that.

Takeaways

*Aleisha Balestri, Jessie Wirkus Haynes, Kayla Urban Fettig, and Liz Angeli reflect on what they've gained from attending WIS as writers, writing educators, and members of different professional communities.

Aleisha: So, 2023 was my first time participating in the Writing Innovation Symposium, and I've actually taken quite a lot away. One, and this is something that I didn't expect, is inspiration beyond the classroom. When we did the Community-Generated Poetry Project, it was something where I really wasn't sure what I was getting into, but the experience was impactful in so many ways. So, I actually talked to the facilitators, Barb and Melissa, and I'm trying to do something similar at COD to represent what students' experiences are.

And something else: My flashtalk was on how a narrative project I teach is a way to kind of vex the space, the tension that's created there. It was a precursor to research I'm doing now on why students are feeling so disengaged with writing and what is happening in their lives that makes this trend continuous. In fact, I just finished a related presentation, which I assumed was going to be mainly for instructors, but the audience ended up being almost all students. So, I asked them to join and share their experience, and it was a very powerful conversation. Now, I want to investigate more, and I would love to see WIS bring students to the forefront and have them speak on this or other topics.

Kayla: The very first WIS I attended was right before the pandemic. As an adjunct, I got the chance to see graduate students talk on panels, and I got to have sidebar conversations about graduate school. WIS was the first conference where I learned how to network and ask questions (maybe too many) and was fully welcomed—and the price for the symposium for graduate students and adjuncts was beyond reasonable. It seemed like the best conference for me to dip my toes in.

Every year I take away something new, whether I can learn from others, network, and build relationships at this symposium or if it helps me reshape how I think I teach and research. It also made me understand what I am passionate about much better than what I thought previously. The evolution from first being an adjunct attendee to a PhD student presenter to one of the only graduate students on the Steering Committee has overwhelmingly made me feel welcomed. People know who I am, what I can do, and what I can advocate for in future WIS symposiums. At the same time, I get the luxury to work with some of the most influential scholars in the field in a capacity that doesn't seem hurried, disingenuous, or forced. It has been one of my favorite symposiums to attach myself to solely due to how positive it leaves me feeling every year.

Liz: What keeps me coming back to WIS is that I feel like it's a playground, and I don't feel like any other conference feels like a playground. I also think this is the only conference where I actually write things up and submit them for publication, maybe because I don't feel like other conferences are places where I can actually think through ideas. The symposium is a space where I feel like I can do that.

So last year for WIS, three of my graduate students and I ran a workshop about discernment mapping, which is an activity I created for a public humanities and career formation graduate class, and we now have an article forthcoming in *Jesuit Higher Education*. My WIS presentations and workshops have been impacting the work I do with communities outside academia. I completed spiritual direction training a couple years ago, and my cohort had our first reunion this past weekend. I was invited to talk about how I'm integrating my spiritual direction training into my academic work, and the symposium showed up twice! This is my favorite thing: One of my teachers from my training program, she's in her late 70s, has been a spiritual director for decades, and is a Dominican nun. She emailed me to see if she could use the discernment map prompt in a workshop she's leading, and I've been invited to do the discernment map for churches, which is really exciting.

Jessie: I love that it's generative, right? Early on, WIS made me understand the collaborative nature of writing and underscored that everyone is a writer. Each of the WISes inspired me to think of writing as social justice or writing as inherently linked to change. Take Danielle Clapham's presentation at WIS 2018, "Space for Every Body: Reading for Access and Inclusion in the First-Year Writing Classroom." I have my students do her spatial analysis every year in my empathy classes for healthcare students. I know we say that teachers steal things, but WIS is a place where we share things.

WIS is also inextricably linked to my ideas about curriculum. When WIS started, Jackielee Derks and I were making a scholarly article database for first-year writing, and that turned into something we presented at the symposium—a tool to help teach writing to students in any discipline. This project represents a core of my pedagogy, of the way I work, trying to make writing this accessible thing for everyone: we're talking about mathematicians as writers, and we're talking about healthcare workers and cinematographers—everyone is a writer. So, for me, I don't feel like the first-year writing curriculum ever died. I feel like it lives forward. And it just gets better and better.

Impact

*Over the years, WIS plenaries have included a presentation by Julie Lindquist and Bump Halbritter (2018), a roundtable facilitated by Maria Novotny (2019), and workshops led by Jessica Edwards (2022) and Barb Clauer and Melissa Kaplan (2023).

Julie: In 2018, Bump Halbritter and I presented "Pedagogical Triage and Troubled Times," which reminds me that the times have been troubled for a very long time. I remember thinking, then, about our curriculum in First-Year Writing at Michigan State and our set of pedagogical moves as a way to address conflict and polarity. I'm realizing now just how responsive that whole occasion felt, just sort of intimate and responsive. I don't think I've seen another conference space that worked like that.

Barb: I hope this doesn't sound how it might sound, but the invitation was such a surprise—and it was such an honor, in the sense that it's such a good thing to have an external voice that we trust say, 'I can see how this might work at WIS, I can see some ideas.' So, it was such a wonderful experience to need to rise to the occasion, which Melissa and I didn't imagine was in our future.

Jessica: I was definitely surprised and excited to receive an invitation from Patrick. It was my first time giving a plenary workshop, so it was a nice exercise intellectually. I definitely took some risks giving the talk as well. I brought music into the conversation and time to write during the session, and there were some other community moments that I ended up peppering through. So, it was definitely not a traditional talk. It was certainly one that required the audience to play, to have lots of interaction with me, which I felt was useful and fit into the symposium at large.

Melissa: Though Barb and I've collaborated since 2017, our very first conference workshop was at the 2022 WIS, followed by Imagining America's 2022 National Gathering, with the WIS 2023 invite in between. That invite was so exciting, and it was cool and challenging to shape, with Jenn's guidance, the plenary for everyone to experience the power of community-generated poetry.

Maria: A theme that I consistently see in the plenaries is how they're all discussing writing from an innovation lens, like innovation is always a part of it. Whether they're talking about that explicitly or not, they're thinking through writing and through invention in some capacity, as well.

Julie: I think that's true, but *innovative* innovation in a way that seems more low stakes, in such a way that you can actually take it in and learn from it, which is a really lovely and refreshing thing to be able to do with a new idea. At the closing "unconference" of the symposium in 2018, we wrote ideas on post-it notes, and then we went around and took inventory. What it said on the post-it note that I put up was that I understand learning to be a kind of loss, because I had been reading Deborah Britzman's work, and I was really excited about that idea. I also thought that that was fairly non-controversial, but it turned out to be controversial! There were good discussions around it, and they just reminded me what it means to have a commonplace in a way that was productive for me in thinking about the 2020 4Cs CFP. I remember that as a formative moment.

Jessica: I was excited by how interactive the sessions were. For the 2022 symposium, one memorable session for me happened to be Barb and Melissa's workshop. I remember very, very vividly actually creating a poem, and then we came together and read it aloud. And I think the idea of creating it together but then also making it come alive together was something that I thought was, really, a super great exercise. It definitely informed my own approaches to community work in my classes, where I'm like, okay, how can we create together and then work to make sure that we model or show what has been created in some way each time?

Barb: That first Poetry Project workshop we did was small but mighty. The poem that you all created you titled "The Beast," and it was with raw material connected to suicide and depression awareness. That was one of one of those large, multidisciplinary projects that the Poetry Project got to be a part of, that Melissa produced. So, all those layers, the layers of interconnectedness that WIS supports is really powerful. Our work for the 2023 plenary workshop was purposefully done anticipating what Dr. Melissa Tayles was going to do in her plenary talk on trauma-informed pedagogy. Being able to weave all that together and have the plenary workshop be a creative expression and exploration of the big concepts that Melissa would explore the day before: I just appreciated that setup and those layers so much.

Melissa: Another way we've layered at Lansing Community College involves theater students reading the poems. For the WIS-created poems, The Comet Project was enlisted, an undergraduate experimental theater troupe at Marquette. They took the workshop poems and in a couple hours, they created something I'd never envisioned: little plays that expanded the power of each poem —and then they performed them for the closing session! It was so moving and wonderful.

Maria: I must also say from a local perspective, and it's not just myself but other colleagues I know at UWM, we are so grateful for WIS. It's just inspiring to have a resource that you can tap into rather accessibly. And you can build a coalition around talking about writing, making arguments about why writing matters, and doing writing work that connects to the community that we're part of. It's just so important and valuable.

Ethos

As members of the Steering Committee and Marquette colleagues, Jenna Green, Lilly Campbell, and Max Gray have a unique set of perspectives on the WIS and local benefits.

Lilly: I really value the ethos of the symposium. I think it's one of the most focused on classroom practices that work and innovation in assignments and in pedagogy. I always leave with new ideas.

Jenna: I appreciate the accessibility of a local, campus conference, but I would say what keeps bringing me back is more than just the convenience. I always feel really rejuvenated, inspired.

Max: Jenna used the word invigorating, and WIS is invigorating or maybe inspiring to me. Also, I'll say as someone whose primary role is not in the classroom, being involved in the symposium has been really useful for me to listen in and continue to learn more about the ways that teachers think about their work and the work of their students, to help me understand what I can do from inside the libraries to support that work.

Lilly: I feel like it's been a place of consistency, when there's been a lot of upheaval. There was too much flux happening in our writing program, so WIS has offered some stability. I also think departmentally we have a lot of siloing between the people that teach our first-year writing course and our full-time faculty. We're doing lots of cool things with writing, and it's really important that we have spaces to share that. On a similar level, I'm thinking about our graduate students and the WIS being a really powerful space for them to see writing research as a kind of research, to think about their classrooms as potential sites for research, to make connections with the UWM program. WIS elevates their classroom work in ways that I think it doesn't get elevated enough.

Jenna: For me, it's also a chance to connect with people at Marquette in different ways. Max and I, we're working on another thing in ways that feel built upon from a kind of history and relationship and trust. And WIS doesn't seem to have a competitive or cutthroat environment at all. It's very welcoming, inclusive, and I think that inspires people to really bring thoughtful ideas and research. Paul Feigenbaum was a plenary, and I remember him talking about the concept of failure. That's something that in my 3210 class I've really adopted. Chris Anson's project, cataloging teaching experiences in the pandemic with 100-word stories, I think that was really generative, too.

Lilly: I think some of the more powerful memories of WIS I have are ones that have created space for reflection on myself, on my teaching practices. I found the trauma-informed pedagogy talk by Melissa Tayles really powerful this year. And I think it was 2022 that Liz Angeli did a discernment activity, where we were doing mapping, that I still have hanging in my office.

Max: I also remember Liz Angeli and her graduate students' session. That was a good example of what is really important about so many folks' contribution to the symposium, which is to call collective attention to the very personal stakes of our writing for us. The pedagogy-oriented space of the symposium is also a very personal space for people. And I think that's really valuable for reminding us all why we do what we do on a daily basis, why we want to show up. Jessica Edwards's keynote from 2022, "Writing to Liberate: On Self, Community, and Meaningfulness," was another great example of really bringing to the forefront the work that our writing can do in our lives and also the lives of others.

Lilly: I was also thinking about our relationship with Bedford/St. Martin's. There's the really awesome dinner, which is always a highlight every year, but there's also the very real way that has put me in contact with publishers and broad conversations that I wouldn't have had before.

Jenna: I also think WIS is this great confidence-building symposium in that way. You're kind of like, 'Oh, okay! I tested reaching out to a publisher. Now I know I can do it again.' So, I think it helps me scaffold as a professional and researcher as well.

Max: I haven't spent the majority of my professional life in libraries. I was a graduate student in literary studies for a number of years, and I was teaching composition. So, dialoguing and sharing ideas with folks at the symposium helps me see more connections between the kind of work I'm doing now, and the different kinds of work I've done in the past. For example, there's a phenomenon that I see on a very regular basis on campus, where I'm trying to support people who are already interested in doing digital work and I'm trying to encourage people who maybe wouldn't have imagined themselves doing that work. At WIS, we've made those kinds of offers to people, and they've actually taken us up, which is a great testament to the very open and supportive space of the symposium. And that's really what we should be trying to support among our communities, you know, across the board: to experiment and do things differently than we would have imagined doing them or the way we've been doing them in the past.

On the Fringe

*In a conversation that spanned higher ed and healthcare, Bump Halbritter, Marie Cleary-Fishman, Kelsey Otero, Paul Feigenbaum, and Seán McCarthy surfaced some of the meanings that innovation has accrued within the WIS community.

Seán: I met Jenn and Paul through the Coalition for Community Writing, and also a colleague of ours, Dawn Opel, and Dawn and I decided to go to WIS to work on an article about innovation. We thought what better place to do it than at an innovation summit of sorts? Paul was the plenary speaker at WIS that year, and Paul and I have been working closely together ever since. So, to me, innovation is relationship-based.

Kelsey: In so many circles I have worked in, there was this notion that innovation was more concentrated in business or engineering or disciplines outside of humanities. And I have always struggled with that, because when it comes to being a good innovator, your ability to communicate, to be creative, and to see connections are the skills I talk about with students, and they are all core things to the humanities, and writing in particular. But it's not always highlighted when you think of innovation. So, I think a lot about that, and how much WIS really shined a spotlight for me on how different groups can recognize and see where inclusive innovation fits.

Marie: Healthcare has a tendency to feel like, you know, our world is the worst, and our situation is the worst. We have the most problems; we're imposed on so much; and funding is bad. And so, you know, we can get kind of lost in our own world. And I find it really helpful—I think that's probably one of the best takeaways I had from the symposium—to hear the perspectives, good and bad, from other fields struggling in similar ways.

Bump: A lot of the work that Julie Lindquist and I have done has been innovative or has attempted to find purchase as innovation. At WIS, I do recall one conversation in particular where Julie and I were talking about something that really motivates an awful lot of our work. That's the concept of learning as loss, which goes back to Deborah Britzman. I remember how resistant people were: Like, I didn't get into this business to be a professor and start thinking about people losing shit. And that was not the first time we'd encountered that. But I mean in this particular instance it was really a memorable thing—at which point we turned our attention mostly towards commonplaces.

Seán: I think when we talk about innovation in a kind of an abstract way, we're thinking of building new things. But I'm now, more and more, seeing it through faith and relationships in the sense that I don't see how we get to do anything together if we don't have trust. And we don't have an openness to it working—or not working. And I think in some ways that WIS in both its structure and the way that it engendered conversation speaks to that kind of faith and openness and trust.

Paul: I'm interested in the way that conversation has evolved. I think increasingly I've come to see trust as the basic *sine qua non* of anything. I think it's the foundation of good teaching, the foundation of community. You can't do anything without trust; you can't really have a society without trust. And I think it's the breakdown of social trust in our general society that is the key contributor to the larger hyperpolarization and mutual hatreds that are going on everywhere.

Kelsey: I'm really big on how innovation doesn't mean brand new. I really like when we talk about innovation as something that creates value for whoever you're trying to solve a problem for. And so I'm always struck, after every symposium, how much value creation there is for the students that get to be the beneficiaries of lessons or conversations that were started at WIS and the ripple effect of how many other people are impacted, not just those who attended. I'm struck by the value creation that emerges from WIS because attendees have a space to build new connections and partnerships.

Marie: I think that if you break things down to a very, very fundamental level in whatever field you're looking at, that applies. If you don't have the right structure—which means people, equipment, resources, knowledge—if you don't have those things, and then you don't have the right processes in place, you can work forever to get an outcome, and you may never get it.

Bump: I think, Marie, there's also a segue between commonplace and structure plus process equals outcome. Because structure and process are commonplaces, right? I was looking over my presentation, and I think about 30 of the 300 slides that Julie and I presented in 30 minutes had the following phrase on it: we learn on the fringe of what we know. And I think that, again, speaks to commonplaces but also this idea that as we innovate, we're on the fringe of what we know. We don't make these sorts of massive leaps. We're always right at the edge of where we are, and those of us who are pointing towards innovation are potentially looking at a different fringe than others to grow. And so bringing those folks around is really tough. I think that's the real work of innovation.

Seán: I think the idea of fringe and periphery is important to what WIS is and the way that it operates. Because, you know, it's porous enough where Marie, who works in the healthcare sector, gets to be a central part of a conversation in a way that, like, if we brought Marie to Cs, that would never happen, right? So, it's the smaller spaces like Community Writing or WIS where I feel like those who are on the fringe of a discipline can find like-minded people. And I really appreciate the WIS for creating that space.

62 | FISHMAN, ET AL.ment>

Conclusion: or, Three Easy Steps to Your Very Own WIS[2]

Jenn Fishman

Ending with a recipe is, to a degree, a feint. After all, small conferences are not easy weekday meals that take just thirty minutes, start to finish, and though WIS has some turnkey components, there is no pre-fab symposium kit. Really, the preceding conversations put it best, offering a dialogic sense of all that is involved in holding a meaningful recurring event. The narrative recipe that follows offers a compromise, a combination of stories, ingredients, and instructions plus one last invitation: to make your own WIS, to join us some time, or to participate in one of the many small conference communities already to be found.

1. *Start with an idea that fills a need and leadership, including core teams.* As Chief Capacitator, I assembled the first local host team. Subsequently, WIS participants formed a volunteer cross-institutional steering committee, and within it, a group of core organizers emerged. Each year, we regroup, and we (re)commit to filling the promises of the next symposium.

2. *Make time an ally by aligning processes with priorities.* We end each symposium by looking ahead and discussing what to keep, change, and add. In May, we meet (online) to brainstorm, guided by the priority we place on people, concrete practices, and creating possibilities. Plans cohere as steering committee members take up and agree to take on different aspects of emerging programing, and by August we have a production calendar and project leads.

3. *Embrace improv, which is not a free-for-all but a deeply rhetorical praxis.* There is always something. The year a polar vortex shut down Marquette's campus, we had 36 hours to revamp before participants arrived. Together, we marshalled all our available knowledge and resources, and the WIS went on. The same spirit drives our planning sessions, where we affirm new ideas with follow-up cues and questions (e.g., yes, say more, who, how, why) that lend themselves to deliberation and, over time, good group decision making.

So far, we have eschewed opportunities to scale up, expand out, and take on partners or sponsors that might significantly change our culture or focus. We have also decided that so far we don't need officers and elections or bylaws and dues to maintain vision, workflow, and integrity. Instead, WIS has an ethos that unites writers and writing educators who share a work ethic along with a sense of ethics that enables us to build and sustain community. In fact, we are currently developing plans for satellite events: think food trucks and cooking classes rather than franchises. Whatever transpires, we look forward to writing and innovating together.

Notes

1. As we explained in the WIS '23 CFP: "Flashtalks give writers and writing educators a chance to share their WISdom in short, snappy presentations meant to spark discussion. In five minutes—and no more— flashtalkers will discuss things they have done (rather than things they plan to do or things they think about). As part of their presentations, flashtalkers are invited to share a single artifact, such as a one-page double-sided handout, a piece of fruit, a half-page infographic, a bumper sticker, or a bookmark."

2. Hungry for more? Find transcripts of the conversations excerpted in this piece and related WIS documentation in the Digital Archive of Literacy Narratives.

Author Bios

Participants are listed alphabetically by first name, following the convention established in the first Writing Innovation Symposium program.

Abigayle Farrier is a graduate instructor at Texas Christian University, where she teaches composition and literature courses. Her research and teaching interests include nineteenth-century transatlantic women's writing, women's literary networks, Antiguan literary production, and the intersections of psychology, pedagogy, and writing.

Aleisha Balestri is an assistant English professor at the College of DuPage where she specializes in teaching first-year writing, emphasizing the interplay between research, digital media, and self-discovery. She also researches how the evolution of technology impacts equity and success within First-Year Composition and how it can be used to uplift student voices.

Barbara Clauer is a professor of English and writing at Lansing Community College. She is also the creator of the Community-Generated Poetry Project, exploring challenging concepts through collaboratively created art.

Bump Halbritter is Associate Professor of Writing and Rhetoric in the Department of Writing, Rhetoric, and American Cultures at Michigan State University. Bump's research, teaching, scholarship, and national service have centered on equitable teaching, learning, and assessment practices, especially with regard to non-traditional literacies, storytelling, audio-visual writing, and informed reflective praxis.

Darci Thoune is First-Year Writing Program Coordinator and Professor of English at the University of Wisconsin–La Crosse where she teaches first-year writing and a range of upper-level writing courses in the writing and rhetoric major. Her teaching, research, scholarship, and public intellectual work span the fields of writing studies and fat studies.

Derek G. Handley is an assistant professor of English at the University of Wisconsin-Milwaukee. His research interests/areas of specialization include African American Rhetoric and Literature, writing studies, rhetorical history, and the Black Freedom Movement.

Elizabeth Angeli, Associate Professor of English at Marquette University and a spiritual director, has worked with prehospital care clinicians and educators to improve healthcare writing training and practice. As a spiritual director, Liz accompanies people on their personal and professional journeys, teaches discernment-based writing classes and workshops, and serves on retreat leadership teams.

Gitte Frandsen, PhD candidate at UW-Milwaukee, researches translingual literacy studies, cultural rhetorics, and transformative praxes in teaching, writing program administration, and writing across the curriculum. Her dissertation focuses on the linguistic superdiversity of transnational students in U.S. writing classrooms.

Holly Burgess is a PhD candidate and instructor at Marquette University. Her research and writing center on African American literature, violence and Black activism, hip-hop, and LGBTQ+ studies. Her dissertation is a literary genealogy of Black social movements and traces how Black activists write, react, and respond to extrajudicial killings.

Jenn Fishman, WIS co-founder and Chief Capacitator, is Associate Professor of English and Co-Director of the Ott Memorial Writing Center at Marquette University. Her teaching, research, scholarship, and national professional service span feminist rhetorics, writing research, undergraduate research in writing studies, and community listening.

Jenna Green is a teaching assistant professor and Assistant Director of Foundations Instruction at Marquette University. Her teaching and research focus on digital and multimodal composing, literacy studies, and multilingual writers.

Jennifer Kontny, WIS steering committee member, is Director of the Writing Program and Associate Professor of English at Mount Mary University. Jennifer's work stretches across multimodal composing, feminist epistemologies, writing programs, quantitative methodologies, and digital narrative.

Jessica R. Edwards, PhD, is Associate Professor of English, Co-Academic Director for the Mandela Washington Fellowship Program, and Writing Internship Coordinator at the University of Delaware. Her teaching, research, service, and scholarship investigate critically conscious pedagogies to encourage thoughtful public writing practices.

Jessie Wirkus Haynes is Assistant Professor of English at Bellin College, specializing in composition, narrative medicine, and DEI work for healthcare students. Her teaching, research, scholarship, and community service focus on collaborative ways to empower students and foster social change through language and the act of writing.

Julie Lindquist is Professor of Rhetoric and Writing and Director of First-Year Writing at Michigan State University. Julie's academic work addresses class identities and working-class language and culture; theories of rhetoric and culture; literacy theories and practices; inclusive and equitable teaching practices; narrative methodologies, and pedagogies of storytelling.

Kaia L. Simon is Associate Professor of English and Director of the Blugold Seminar Writing Program at the University of Wisconsin, Eau Claire. Her teaching, research, service, and administrative work span transnational literacy studies, feminist rhetorics, critical Hmong studies, and rhetoric and composition.

Kayla Urban Fettig, a Mount Mary University adjunct and University of Milwaukee-Wisconsin PhD student, attended the last three WISes. Her communities include GTAs, adjuncts, and other contingent laborers; first-year writers and writing teachers, and the Milwaukee-based non-profit The Community.

Kelsey Otero is the Senior Director of Community Engagement at Marquette University. She works to build meaningful bi-directional partnerships, collaborate on new social impact initiatives (such as the WIS), and strategically connect resources between the Milwaukee community and the Marquette campus.

Lilly Campbell is Associate Professor of English at Marquette University where she oversees the Foundations in Rhetoric course. Her teaching and research focus on feminist rhetorics, rhetorics of health and medicine, and technical and professional communication.

Louise Zamparutti is Assistant Professor of English at the University of Wisconsin-La Crosse. Her research and teaching take a social justice approach to technical communication, challenging normative assumptions of objectivity and incorporating historically underrepresented authors and audiences into the development of student writing.

Margaret Perrow is Professor and Chair of English at Southern Oregon University. As director of the Oregon Writing Project at SOU, she works closely with teachers at all stages of their careers; her research interests include teachers' professional identities and ELA pedagogy.

Maria Novotny, Assistant Professor of English at the University of Wisconsin-Milwaukee, collaborates with fertility providers and advocates on coalitional efforts with the Building Families Alliance of Wisconsin. Her research integrates storytelling and other creative practices as tools for reproductive healthcare advocacy. Her collection *Infertilities, A Curation* will feature such work.

Marie Cleary-Fishman is a nurse and Vice President, Clinical Quality for the American Hospital Association (AHA). Her strategic vision led to the formalization of the Funded Partnership work unit which writes for, obtains, and executes grants and contracts to support the AHA and member strategic priorities, including utilization of Quality Improvement concepts and methods.

Maxwell Gray is a digital scholarship librarian in Raynor Memorial Libraries at Marquette University. He is a member of the Writing Innovation Symposium's steering committee, where he supports multimodal research displays.

Melissa Kaplan, multidisciplinary arts producer, is Academic and Arts Outreach Coordinator at Lansing Community College, Lansing, MI. She creates, facilitates and promotes programs and events that engage the arts with other disciplines, exploring a wide range of social issues.

Patrick W. Thomas is Associate Professor and Director of Undergraduate Studies in English at the University of Dayton. His teaching and scholarship focus on digital composition, social media, and empirical research methods.

Paul Feigenbaum is Associate Professor of English at Florida International University and Co-Editor of the *Community Literacy Journal*. His scholarship, teaching, and community engagement currently focus on transdisciplinary problem-solving, generative failure, engaged listening, and prison literacy.

Sara Heaser is an associate teaching professor who studies, teaches, and writes about first-year writing Her writing has been published in *Composition Studies, The Journal of the Scholarship of Teaching and Learning,* and on *The Mind Hears,* a blog by and for deaf and hard-of-hearing academics. She is a steering committee member for the Writing Innovation Symposium.

Seán McCarthy is a professor in the School of Writing, Rhetoric & Technical Communication and Director of the Cohen Center for the Humanities at James Madison University. He pursues impact-focused transdisciplinary projects with local nonprofits and nonprofit funders, regional and national government departments, private companies, think tanks, and other universities.

JAMAL: Adult Literacy Decolonizing Knowledge and Activism in 1970s Jamaica

Randi Gray Kristensen

Abstract

In the summer of 1978, at Church Teachers College in Mandeville, Jamaica, a class of advanced students participating in the Jamaica Movement for the Advancement of Literacy (JAMAL) wrote, cast, rehearsed, and performed a play that satirized several major institutions—the family, the church, and the business sector—as well as class and gender relations. This essay locates this nearly forgotten event in the context of the opportunities JAMAL offered for decolonizing knowledge and activism for poor and working-class Jamaicans. The reactions the play provoked on the micro and macro levels help to explain JAMAL's subsequent trajectory, which follows the broader trajectory of the conflicting visions for the purposes of adult education in Jamaica's pre- and post-Independence era: from the efforts of Jamaica Welfare starting in the 1930s through active decolonization in the 1970s, through global and local institutional neglect in the 1980s, to contemporary insertion into the neo-liberal global economy. Recovering this instance of popular education and performance illuminates both gaps in the historical record and possible foundations for reinvention in the 21st Century.

In the summer of 1978, at Church Teachers' College in Mandeville, Jamaica, a class of advanced students participating in the Jamaica Movement for the Advancement of Literacy (JAMAL) wrote, cast, rehearsed, and performed a play that satirized several major institutions—the family, the church, and the business sector—as well as class and gender relations. The students reconstructed everyday experiences into a narrative that not only depicted how literacy empowered the normally disenfranchised to overcome structures of repression, but also challenged the expectations of the program and its administrators.

Here, I hope to locate this nearly forgotten event in the context of the opportunities JAMAL offered for decolonizing knowledge and activism for poor and working-class Jamaicans. I will briefly analyze the reactions it provoked on the micro and macro levels, through JAMAL's subsequent decline and recent reinvention as the Jamaica Foundation for Lifelong Learning. JAMAL's trajectory follows the broader trajectory of conflicting visions for the purposes of adult education in the pre- and post-Independence era: from the efforts of Jamaica Welfare starting in the 1930s through active decolonization in the 1970s, through global and local institutional neglect in the 1980s, to contemporary insertion into the neo-liberal global economy. Recovering this instance of popular education and performance illuminates both gaps in the historical record and possible foundations for reinvention in the 21st Century.

The question of archive and authority is a pressing one in Caribbean Studies, where the traditional archive contains the records of imperial conquest, human trafficking, and exploitation, but the record of those who were conquered, trafficked, and exploited remains fragmented, dispersed, oral, and full of gaps (Thomas 27). For this work, I am interweaving imperfect recollection, i.e., myself as archive, with historical records, family history, and academic theory. There are moments where these elements intersect gracefully, and others where they collide and clash against each other, reflecting the uneven processes of decolonizing knowledge and activism in the academy. In short, there is much more to be said about who and what is legible and illegible, to whom, and why.

Our Story

Summer 1978, Mandeville, Manchester, Jamaica. My mother has sent me home to Jamaica from the States to my uncle's house for "turning into too much of a damn Yankee," and under the pretense that I will be my grandmother's physical therapist as she recovers from foot surgery. But working with Grandma takes a grand total of about a half hour every day. That leaves a lot of time for a teenager to occupy.

On the television, there are recurring ads for something called JAMAL. I am literate, seventeen, and have completed two years of community college. I find out that the nearest JAMAL classes are offered at Church Teachers' College, so I walk over to volunteer. The administrator says I don't have the training to teach the literacy classes, but they are looking for a cultural activity for the advanced students. Would I write a play about why it was important to learn how to read and write, and the students could perform it? OK, I say, and walk home.

I am excited, but also completely daunted. I have no idea why somebody would choose to read and write, because it had never been a choice for me. I was automatically enrolled in school at a certain age and expected to become literate. So, I think, well, let me ask the people who actually had to answer that question before enrolling in JAMAL.

A JAMAL staff member introduces me as a volunteer from the States, and I am left on my own. I explain that I have Jamaican roots and attended Bishop's—a local girls' school—for a couple years, am home for the summer, and am looking forward to working on this project with them. Our group is small, maybe ten to fifteen people. I share the charge: a play about why reading and writing is important. I invite each person to say why they had come to JAMAL and ask if we could build a play from that together. The oldest lady—Grandma's age—says she wants to be able to read her Bible for herself. A Rasta, younger than me, wants to qualify to go to a high school. Several young women, slightly older than me, want to qualify for office jobs. The older Rasta agrees with the elder lady: Bible-reading is a goal. I'm sure there are other reasons for gaining greater literacy, but my memory hasn't held on to them.

Over the course of the next month, we come up with a plot, cast characters, write a script and learn lines, assemble props and costumes, and make flyers to advertise the one-time performance. The JAMAL administrators—maybe teacher trainers or teachers in training at the Teachers' College where the project is housed—pretty much leave us alone; we call on them for help with furnishing the stage, but that is about it. This is a no-budget enterprise.

The administrators must have heard about the play because they ask to attend a rehearsal. What they see is a classic farce. I don't remember characters' names, but let's say Dulcimina is our illiterate hero. She works as a helper, the recently adopted polite title for maid, in the household of a businessman and his wife. She is constantly making errors, like mistaking the salt for sugar, or not buying the right things at the shop, because she can't read the list the wife has made. Things get more complicated when it turns out that Pastor is having an affair with the businessman's wife, and our Dulcimina is supposed to be passing the right notes between them about when to meet up while also fending off the amorous attentions, or what we call now the sexual harassment, of the businessman himself. The upshot is that the businessman catches the pastor with his wife, and Dulcimina somehow extracts a bag of money to go to JAMAL so she will have better choices about how and where to make a living. At least, I think that's how it ended. Alas, I no longer have a copy of the script.

The administrators can't help but laugh, but they are also a bit horrified. This is not a respectability narrative; rather, it satirizes several institutions that a properly literate person should be aspiring to: marriage, middle-class household, business, church. Still, it is too late to write a new play, and they must admit that it meets the stated mission. They did make one casting request: perhaps the Rasta could be the businessman instead of the pastor. We agree to that. The performance goes on. It is recorded by the Jamaican Broadcasting Corporation for future broadcast—I don't know if that ever happened—and a good time is had by all.

Our play's co-authors envisioned having more choices, having more agency, and being less vulnerable to the institutions and their attendant literacies, such as schools, banking, and the church, as a basic goal. Thus, literacy was important because it offered more choices than illiteracy. The co-authors of the play did not need literacy to think, to have relationships, to raise children, to be creative, to worship God, to work, or to live their lives. But literacy offered more ways to go about doing those things, and new forms of expression, such as writing a play together that critiqued the middle-class respectability politics. It also made possible other ways of earning a living if jobs could be found.

The play's composition process is recognizable to those familiar with the work of Jamaica's Sistren Theatre Collective and Augusto Boal's Theatre of the Oppressed. As one critic notes:

> In the Jamaican context, theatre...involved addressing the injustices of neo/colonialism. Those who had previously been silenced by Jamaica's colonial system were given the opportunity to express the latent anger that had accumulated through centuries of oppression and, through observing themselves

in performance, to understand their past subject formation under oppressive regimes. (Smith 238)

I had come to the play composition process through the oppressive regime of childhood. Boarding school at Bishop's was boring. As a troop of nine-year-olds, we entertained ourselves by making up skits to songs by Tom Jones or based on characters in TV shows. We also regularly roasted our teachers and headmistress. We inherited and embellished an underground school song, sung to the tune of "My Darling Clementine":

> Come to Bishop's, come to Bishop's,
> For a life of misery.
> There's a signpost on the corner
> Saying "Welcome Unto Thee."
> Don't believe it, don't believe it,
> Cuz it's just a pack of lies.
> If it wasn't for the teachers
> We would be in Paradise.
> Build a bonfire, build a bonfire,
> Put Skemps [the headmistress] at the top.
> Put the teachers in the middle
> And burn the (bleeping) lot.

Collaborative and critical play-making was the only kind I knew, informed by my Jamaican classmates and our experiential understanding of the power dynamics of a colonizing Anglophile boarding school.

Forty-one years later, in 2019, I wrote and performed an earlier version of this essay as a reflection *about* a community writing project/workshop *for* a community *reflecting on* community. The workshop where I debuted this piece, "Decolonization, Social Movements, and Performance in the Caribbean 1968-1988," was organized at York University, Toronto, Canada, by Caribbean activist-scholars Professors Honor Ford-Smith, Ronald Cummings, and B. Anthony Bogues. The workshop gathered several generations of cultural workers, activists, and academics, many of us wearing all three hats. It was a hybrid space where those of us who have been crossing national borders, languages, roles, and audiences knew that this time we were performing for each other, and so there was a tremendous freedom to bring our whole fractal selves into dialogue, to reflect on an era of collaborations and hopes and failures, and to extract what was still useful and had promise for the future. Thus, this essay builds on the themes of the workshop to illustrate decoloniality as a complex process taking place in and between the individual, the community, the nation-state and its institutions, history, and performance.

Jamaica Welfare

Mandeville in 1978 is not home for my grandmother and me. We are at my uncle's house because Grandma can no longer live alone at her house in Seville Heights, Priory, St. Ann, the only home in Jamaica I truly recall. A half-acre with a two-bedroom house, three mango trees, four coconut trees, one guava, one lime, one pimento, one breadfruit, banana, chicken wire fencing strung with red and gungo peas, numberless chickens, and one bad dog. Supposedly Grandma's little and productive half-acre was part of the first housing scheme established in Jamaica by barrister, labor activist, and statesman Norman Manley. Could be, since one of the streets in the area is named for him.

Housing schemes like Seville Heights emerged from efforts to institutionalize decoloniality via the organizing of Jamaica Welfare, whose program was education and economic development on the co-op model of shared ownership by workers and participants. In 1969, Sybil Francis complicates Phillip Sherlock's 1949 history of the founding of Jamaica Welfare in the late 1930s. Sherlock describes a gentleman's agreement between Norman Manley and the president of United Fruit to donate one cent per stem of bananas to fund the programs of Jamaica Welfare. Francis argues that Jamaica Welfare's origins actually emerge from discontent and agitation among the independent banana growers and the banana plantation workers, who had to rely on a monopoly market —United Fruit—for their product. Both groups argued that they were underpaid for their labors. Thus, she restores the agency of both groups as instigators of the grievances that Norman Manley's championing of Jamaica Welfare is supposed to address.

The program's initial model involved building staffed community centres to provide an "educational and recreational programme for the improvement of rural life in all its respects" (Francis 45), including literacy classes. But it soon became clear to Jamaica Welfare administrators that the community centre model reproduced relationships of paternalism that contradicted the goals of community self-help. The community centre model was sidelined, and Jamaica Welfare shifted to using existing structures—for example, schools and churches=for community groups led by local leaders. Jamaica Welfare supported local efforts with project grants and outside expertise. Vincent George records the success of the more grassroots approach to community development: "After only 11 years of existence, the efforts of Jamaica Welfare...had resulted in the formation of 1,180 organised groups, 183 savings unions and a Fisherman's Federation and had embraced 236 villages" (275). Francis describes a "spirit of excitement and challenge which accompanied the birth of nationalism in Jamaica...The Community Development movement developed a strong emotional content" (47). In this way, Jamaica Welfare's efforts became tied to the emergence of the nation-state, and the expectations of working-class Jamaicans for what an independent nation can offer. However, despite the successes, the promise of self-governance on the local level, with national support, was not to be fulfilled by the emerging nation-state. Between the 1940s and the 1960s, community development in Jamaica shifted from this decolonizing and successful bottom-up model to full government and ministerial responsibility, "professionalization," and bureaucratic infrastructure by the time of national independence in 1962. In the wake of those developments, many, if not most, of the community councils disappeared.

By the time I get to Grandma's yard as a little girl in the late 1960s, she has achieved the Jamaica Welfare goals: a solid house of her own, literacy to correspond with her overseas children, and nutritional well-being from her own little property. But I don't recall community involvement beyond her immediate neighbors and her church, and there is no obvious aid for the squatter's village that has come up around the bend.

By the time we get to my uncle's yard in the late 1970's, there has been a sea change. Since Norman Manley "gave" my grandmother her house, "no one name Manley could do any wrong." His son Michael is now Prime Minister, elected on a campaign of democratic socialism, trying to navigate a path between the US and the USSR, two supremely self-interested and antagonistic superpowers, while pursuing as national government policy the recognizable mission of Jamaica Welfare: an "educational and recreational programme for the improvement of rural [and urban] life in all its respects." As part of that program, Manley invigorates JAMAL.

JAMAL

While efforts had previously been made to address the functional illiteracy of nearly half of the Jamaican people, the Manley government declared the eradication of illiteracy urgent, one of the top ten priorities in the 1973 national development plan. In 1974, JAMAL was formed. Its aims were to:

1. Eradicate illiteracy in Jamaica within the shortest possible period.

2. Improve the literacy skills of the adult population of Jamaica.

3. Develop human resources and so enable each adult citizen to participate meaningfully in the social, economic, and cultural development of the country (Miller 13).

The educational goals of the program had thirteen elements: Identity and Self Image, Citizenship and Government, Consumer Education, Community, Continuing Education, Home and Family, Health and Hygiene, Nutrition, Food Production, Occupation, Work, Communication, and Inquiry and Critical Thinking (Miller 15). If we understand decolonization as "ongoing struggles to transform the unequal legacies of racial colonialism and to reconstitute ways of knowing, acting and being" (Ford-Smith), we can trace a narrative of decolonizing educational efforts starting and restarting from the founding of Jamaica Welfare to the founding of JAMAL. We can also note the complicated origins of such efforts in private-public collaborations reliant for their material resources on donations from the state and private donors.

While such educational efforts often claim that the content and actual enactment of such projects' aims will come from the people they are intended to serve, there are definite, if unspoken, barriers in place. Such barriers include program donor or administrator assumptions about learners—that learners differ culturally according to a deficit model, which positions donors or administrators as role models. In effect, even in situations where the discourse is supposed to be learner-driven, a soft colonialism often prevails. There can be a whiff of the "civilizing mission" about such programs, whether foreign or domestic, that seeks to devalue learners' own ways of knowing or thinking or doing in the name of "improvement."

Our play's co-authors had their own ideas about how literacy would improve their lives. I don't know what would have happened if we had decided that our play would be about how literacy enables organizing a revolution. That didn't come up as a theme because the students had a sophisticated understanding of their context, which did not in that historical moment include any immediate possibility of revolution. Further, they knew exactly what JAMAL was intended to prepare them for, and they knew just as exactly the limitations of this brave, supposedly new, world. Thus, they chose to reveal their critical knowledge about that.

I would argue that the ordinary Jamaican people who are targets of these "improvement" schemes are always already aware of their positioning vis-a-vis supposed efforts to include them in "modernity." We have, in fact, been part of modernity since our ancestors were shipped as economic cargo from Africa to the Caribbean, and when we entered the factory economies of the plantation. The dissonance between the supposed civilization of colonial ideology and the lived experience of being its disposable labor is never forgotten. Hence the abandonment of the plantations by, first, the Maroons, and then the newly-freed Jamaicans, and the sophisticated calibration of when and where to enter these improvement schemes. When Jamaica Welfare builds and staffs community centres, the people enter them as institutions belonging to Jamaica Welfare and use them for handouts, better known as reparations. When Jamaica Welfare abandons that model and meets the people on the people's own ground, a space is opened for collaboration and cooperation. When JAMAL is founded, it meets its learners where they are: The Rastas are not required to cut their locks, the curriculum materials reflect ordinary Jamaican life, and we are left to devise our own performances.

In the brief decolonizing interlude of mid-1970s Jamaica, we were able to perform a critique of colonial institutions and ideologies that we understood we would enter to meet our unmet material needs. But we wanted the audience and the teachers to know this was not a wholesale embrace. We knew the cracks in the facades, and that the middle class literacies and institutions we were being invited to were no better than we were, even if that was how their members and advocates imagined themselves. In the decolonial sense, our knowledge was coming with us, and we would perform, as in act out AND act up, given the opportunity. Beverly Bell, introducing *Walking on Fire*, a collection of testimonies by Haitian women who survived their country's 1990s military dictatorship, revises the traditional definition of resistance. Drawing on Danny Yee's discussion of James C. Scott's "Anthropology Informs Political Economy," she notes that the traditional definition of resistance demands four things: that it must "be organized and collective," "be principled and selfless," "have revolutionary impact," and "negate the basis of domination." Bell adds a fifth element: that resistance also includes holding the line (5), until such time as greater action becomes possible. So, while our play and our composition process did not negate the basis of domination, we did expose it, and, as a form of resistance, prevent it from making additional inroads.

Two Codas

Coda #1: JAMAL. After structural adjustment and neoliberalism came into play, JAMAL went through a period of subsequent decline and has recently been reinvented as the Jamaica Foundation for Lifelong Learning (JFLL). JFLL is in line with global neoliberalism's goals. JFLL's "community education" aspect promises that "Communities where JFLL Community programmes have been implemented have often been able to realize tangible improvements in employability and an increased and improved participation in governance...This turns communities into 'economic opportunity' zones as learners transition to the worlds of work and entrepreneurship" (Jamaica Foundation for Lifelong Learning). Unfortunately, Inquiry and Critical Thinking, Identity, and Self Image are no longer foregrounded, as they were at JAMAL in 1978. We are once more only interesting or useful to society for the labor we provide for capitalism to capitalize on.

Coda #2: Grandma Gray. At the back of the house, Grandma had a standpipe over a square concrete basin. Some mornings, we would go outside to find a huge toad sunk down in the basin, drawn in the night by the water but unable to jump out in the daylight. Grandma would sprinkle a little salt on it, to dull it, then lift it up on the tines of the garden rake, carry it to the back of the yard, and fling it over the fence onto what she called "Seville Property." She always seemed to take a special glee in that. Sometimes she would let me do the throwing. Much later in life, I came to find out that as a young girl Grandma had worked at Seville Property for the overseer's family as a "butleress." When she had to be in the presence of the mistress of the house, she was forced to hide her hands under her apron, so that their delicate sensibilities would not be offended by the signs of her hard work. Half a century later, she was living in her own house on property carved out of Seville Plantation for her benefit, and still had enough strength in those hands, which now worked for herself and whoever she sought to benefit, to fling unwanted toads over her fence onto her now-neighbor's property. This, too, is performance. As I noted at the start, there are more things to be said about what and who are legible and illegible. But who feels it knows it.

Acknowledgments

With thanks to Tanya L. Shields and Vincent Portillo for their close readings and suggestions that helped shape and develop this essay.

Works Cited

Bell, Beverly. *Walking on Fire: Haitian Women's Stories of Survival and Resistance*, Cornell UP, 2013. *ProQuest Ebook Central*, https://ebookcentral.proquest.com/lib/gwu/detail.action?docID=3138514.

Ford-Smith, Honor. Unpublished brief for invited participants in Decolonization, Performance and Social Movements in the Caribbean and Canada workshop, York University, Toronto, Canada, July 2019.

Francis, Sybil. "The Evolution of Community Development in Jamaica (1937-1962)." *Caribbean Quarterly*, vol. 15, no. 2/3, 1969, pp. 40–58. www.jstor.org/stable/40653111.

George, Vincent. "Reviews Section." *Community Development Journal*, vol. 31, no. 3, 1996, pp. 274–78. http://www.jstor.org/stable/44257287

Jamaica Foundation For Lifelong Learning, https://www.jfll.gov.jm/home/index.php/workplace/community-education. Accessed 12 October 2019.

Miller, Harry, Samuel Thompson, Charles Greer, John Reynolds. "Adult-Literacy Education in Jamaica." *Adult Education Service Center*. U of Southern Illinois, Carbondale. ERIC 178174. September 1979, pp 1-25

Sherlock, Philip. "Experiment In Self-Help." *Caribbean Quarterly*, vol. 1, no. 4, 1949, pp. 31–34. *JSTOR*, www.jstor.org/stable/40652479.

Smith, Karina. "Narratives of Success, Narratives of Failure: The Creation and Collapse of Sistren's 'Aesthetic Space.'" *Modern Drama*, vol. 51, no. 2, 2008, pp. 234–58, http://muse.jhu.edu/journals/modern_drama/v051/51.2.smith.html.

Thomas, Deborah A. "Caribbean Studies, Archive Building, and the Problem of Violence." *Small Axe: a Journal of Criticism*, vol. 17, no. 2, 2013, pp. 27–42, https://doi.org/10.1215/07990537-2323301.

Author Bio

Randi Gray Kristensen, MFA., Ph.D., is Assistant Professor of University Writing at the George Washington University, where she is also affiliate faculty in Africana Studies and Women's, Gender, and Sexuality Studies. She is co-editor of *Writing Against the Curriculum: Anti-Disciplinarity in the Writing and Cultural Studies Classroom* (2009). In addition to scholarly publications in writing studies, she regularly publishes fiction and poetry that draw on her Jamaican heritage. She is presently writing a book amplifying Caribbean artists' critiques of humanitarianism as a remedy for disaster capitalism.

Issues in Community Literacy

Rhetorical Considerations for Missy, an LGBTQ+ Zine at the University of Mississippi

Tyler Gillespie

Abstract

In fall 2019, students at the University of Mississippi began the process of starting the university's first creative publication for/by LGBTQ+ students and allies. Over the course of two years, I helped these students plan, create, and produce their zine. These kinds of texts promote identity-formation and help students feel a greater connection to campus as they see the coexistence of their embodied identities within their academic community. Early in our production process, I realized our localized context presented certain theoretical, ethical, and practical issues in the formation of this counterpublic. Because of the function of counterpublics, *Missy*'s early editorial discussions centered on audience and means of circulation. This personal reflection explores literacy practices connected to our publication of a queer zine in a conservative part of the country.

Keywords: queer literacy, zine, student publication, counterpublic, reflection

Zine-troduction

In fall 2019, I attended a workshop on using zines in community writing classes at a conference hosted by the University of Mississippi (UM). The workshop leaders Don Unger and Liz Lane placed self-published zines along with scissors and stickers on tables for participants to collaborate on a zine. The genre is rooted in a DIY culture of assemblage, and a lot of zines, like the one we made in this workshop, mix modalities like hand-drawn images, texts, comics, cut-outs, and found objects. I had made my first zine over a decade earlier with an artist/psychic/comedian in Chicago, and I returned to them at various points in my life to publish creative work for/with my communities.

Stephen Duncombe traces the lineage of zines to alternative presses in the United States and asserts they became a distinct form in the 1930s when members of the science fiction community created "fanzines." He notes another "defining influence on modern-day zines" occurred four decades later in the mid-70s with punk rock music and fanzines for the counter-cultural movement (7). Creators from other social and political groups soon began to publish similar texts which de-emphasized the "fan" aspect. In the 1980s, zines helped certain queer communities establish themselves. Zines provide spaces for "personal exploration and growth" and community formation as members come "together around zines, learning and growing together" (Quint). This discourse circulated during the AIDS crisis when the LGBTQ+ community faced heavy stigma. The genre created alternative spaces for queer people to express their identities, desires, and futures.

The UM Pride Network's president wanted to create a similar space for LGBTQ+ students on the flagship campus. He attended the conference's zine workshop, and it inspired him to start one at the university. UM had made strides toward inclusivity, but some queer students expressed discomfort on campus. He thought a zine would increase visibility, and I agreed to help him with the publication, which the editorial team later named *Missy*. The name functioned as a sassy rhetorical move to queer the university's problematic nickname Ole Miss, which Ellie Campbell writes is a "reference to the mistress of a plantation." Throughout this reflection, I'll use the collective we, but, as the advisor, I refrained from voting on decisions for it to remain a student-led project. This personal reflection traces the zine's trajectory and situates its ethos into a history of literacies in LGBTQ+ communities. There aren't many LGBTQ+ specific publications for students in the Deep South, so I hope a discussion of our work can add to conversations on the ways educators and other stakeholders can help such students create spaces for community-building and counterpublics in their localized contexts.

After the UM Pride Network president approached me with the idea for *Missy*, we recruited Michael Martella, a native Mississippian who, at the time, was a Creative Writing MFA candidate in poetry. He had lived in Oxford for nine years and agreed that queer students needed a publication to build community through art and writing. "The campus can sometimes feel stifling and like a difficult place to find community," he said during a panel discussion at a conference. "There are a lot of ways for heteronormative students to find community, but not so much for queer students." Diverse queer souths—full of life and love—exist, but there weren't many spaces for LGBTQ+ students to explore issues related to their sexuality.

Early in our production process, I realized our localized context presented certain theoretical, ethical, and practical issues in our formation of a counterpublic. Michael Warner writes that the circulation of text creates a type of public, and textual circulation by/for marginalized groups constitutes a counterpublic. These counterpublics center non-dominant subjectivities and allow for specific discourse to emerge in ways it often can't in more visible spaces. Warner gives the example of a queer counterpublic where "no one is in the closet," so "the presumptive heterosexuality that constitutes the closet for individuals in ordinary speech is suspended" (86). Counterpublics allow for alternative discourse to emerge and can help individuals find community. Historically, these spheres have created "parallel discursive arenas" where subordinated groups can have in-group discussions about "their needs, objectives, and strategies" (Fraser 66). Fraser describes these arenas as subaltern counterpublics and claims they provide a necessary space for marginalized subjectivities to express identities. These are powerful spaces, but they are also risky. The circulation of alternative discourse into a more general audience can potentially have harmful effects.

Because of the function of counterpublics, *Missy*'s early editorial discussions centered on audience and means of circulation. This personal reflection, then, documents our process of bridge-building and explores literacy practices connected to our publication of a queer zine in a conservative part of the country. The textual data I present includes drafts of various public documents like the mission statement and call for submissions. I also incorporate statements Michael Martella made during a conference panel I moderated on the zine.

Missy: Goals

Missy's early editorial meetings often centered on issues of identity and context. The history of queer world-making through zines shaped the way I approached these conversations, specifically as it relates to practical and ethical issues in terms of content. Many queer zines published sexually explicit work. We wanted to cultivate an ethos aware of the history of dissent in queer zines/writing, but we needed to think about the lived realities of current and former students in Mississippi.

These conversations were difficult for me because I hadn't had such frank conversations with students about sexual literacy and because I had to balance my competing subjectivities as a writer and advisor. The writer-in-me didn't want to censor students in any way while the advisor-in-me felt a responsibility to consider the harm a submission could potentially cause. A few of the *Missy* contributors, for example, wanted to use a pseudonym because they feared repercussions either from their home community or larger campus networks.

Mission Statement

Although we initially envisioned *Missy* as a counterpublic specifically for LGBTQ+ students, the editorial team decided to open submissions to allies. Kathy Obear suggests straight people can "be powerful allies and use their privilege to combat individual, cultural, and institutional homophobia and heterosexism" (62). The editorial team decided the inclusion of allies could help contributors who might be in the process of coming out. A queer contributor could claim allyship if confronted by someone for their piece in *Missy*. The move provided both a space for contributors in various stages of coming out as well as for allies to submit work in an act of solidarity. "The goal in all of our discussions was to provide a space for queer students to put their art into the world and establish a sense of community," said Michael, "but we also wanted to make an impact on the larger community, which takes building bridges and making connections." These discussions of audience and rhetorical ecology were some of the most nuanced I've had with students. I'd like to now excerpt an exchange from my interview with Michael as it materializes complex issues connected to the publication's goals and mission statement.

Michael: We had so many intense and complicated conversations about these things. The goal in all of our discussions was to try to not only provide a space for queer students to bring their art into the world and to support one another and love one another and establish a sense of community but also to do some form of outreach and to actually make an impact on the larger community, which takes building bridges and making connections outside of our queer community.

One of the ways we thought to do that was to bring in the voices of allies, non-queer students who may have things to say relative to the content of our publication and our interest in hosting different perspectives. Our opinion was that the more perspectives we could bring in—within reason, obviously—the better able we'd be to facilitate a dialogue that might bridge these disparate communities we wanted to bring together. We wanted to make it such that it wasn't just a queer bubble we were creating but a queer community engaged with people outside of itself, and in so doing, hopefully etching ourselves into this broader community at large. We wanted to do those two things at the same time, which is hard to do.

In this exchange, I'm struck by the nuanced discussion of queer community and literacy practices. Michael believed the publication helped "etch ourselves into the broader community," and articulated the difficulty of providing a space for queer people to be authentically themselves. These are ongoing and complicated conversations many LGBTQ+ organizations must address. Although we couldn't fully resolve some of these issues, we were able to create a mission statement grounded in our literacy practices and connected to our goals of community building. In our mission statement, we described the publication as by/for members of the LGBTQ+ community and allies to that community, but we said submitted work does not need to be LGBTQ+ related as such a stipulation may restrict creative expression. We determined the Masthead would be conscious of our various audiences in the selection of published pieces and noted "historically, queer writing and queer rhetorical modes often challenge accepted norms through subversion," so "selection decisions will avoid censorship of the community" but will consider "any harm a piece could bring to the community if published."

Submissions

Our conversations on writing, queer history, and mediums of queer text encouraged us to be expansive in our call for "poetry, short fiction, creative nonfiction, graphic narratives, fan fiction, satire, interviews, manifestos, reviews, visual art, photography, collage, drawings, and anything else fit to print" ("Call for Submissions"). As many LGBTQ+ communities use the internet to spread text like ezines, we also envisioned an online space for "video and audio submissions—podcast segments, readings, twines, visual performances, etc."

We circulated our original call for submissions in spring 2020, then put *Missy* on pause after the COVID-19 outbreak. At the time, we had six students on the editorial team, but when we came back together in fall 2021, our original crew was down to two. Some folks graduated or became overwhelmed with other responsibilities.

Our team may have dwindled, but *Missy*'s spirit didn't.

We had received enough submissions to produce an issue, and the editorial conversations we had about representation were similarly present in these submissions. Many submissions explored identities through text and art. We published a short story titled "Destruction of Eden," drawings of socially constructed/obstructed bodies, and an essay about the self-expression a student found through a hair journey. "We want to represent the queer community as a complex and nuanced group of people," said Michael. "That's been our agenda from the beginning."

A photo series submission connected to our goal of representation as it showed members of Mississippi's LGBTQ+ community living their everyday lives. The portraits show images of students in public spaces, living and laughing. These types of images are important for students who enroll at the university who might feel their queerness means they won't be able to laugh much on campus. We chose one of these portraits for the cover because it speaks to the series' goals and directly centers students.

The editorial board contemplated choosing a different portrait: a particularly joyful image of a student at a party. We ultimately didn't choose the party portrait for the cover because the underage student held a beer in it. The image led us to think deeply about how a cover image frames the content within a zine. We worried the circulation of the image might cause the student harm and misrepresent our intentions. "There's more weight to the cover," said Michael, "and in producing and publishing art, there are ethical considerations to the decisions we make."

Figure 1. Cover, *Missy: LGBTQ+ Literary Magazine at the University of Mississippi*. Photo credit: Hooper Schultz.

Missy: Resources

We originally wanted to create physical copies of the zine, but we decided to create a digital-only first issue to minimize costs and because we thought a digital format might be more appropriate for our audience. Queer communities have, historically, used the internet to organize in/through digital spaces and create counterpublics. Megan Opperman posits digital spaces, like Tumblr, have enabled members of the LGBTQ+ community to "blur the lines between private and public" and create queer spaces "in opposition to the status quo" (68). Similarly, we hoped the digital publication would create an "oppositional" space, so we uploaded the first issue to the free electronic publishing platform Issuu.

We created the issue digitally, but we still wanted to enact the materiality of traditional zines. To do this, we created two versions of stickers with the QR code for the issue. We also thought this format spoke to student culture as they often put stickers on their laptops in a rhetorical move to publicly display aspects of their identity or beliefs.

Figure 2. Sticker with QR code for Issue 1.

I'll briefly discuss the process for the *Missy* planet sticker. Michael had hand drawn a planet in his notebook, and then I took a photo of it with my phone and digitally edited it. An artist friend of mine then helped manipulate the image for printing. He'd made sticker art before, so he helped me edit the image, choose the background, place the QR code, and print the sticker. We bought 110 high-quality stickers for $150. The stickers were a big hit at the release party discussed in the next section, and we only had a few remaining after our issue launch.

Custom stickers may be a good option for publications that want to keep costs down and still produce a material artifact. The QR code is an important rhetorical feature on these stickers as it sends people to the actual text. These stickers were a lot of fun to make and seemed to connect to the aesthetic and ethos of our target audience.

Missy: Relationships

University Partnerships

We wanted to produce a print run, so to cover costs we secured partnerships with the university's Department of Writing & Rhetoric (DWR), the Sarah Isom Center for Women and Gender Studies, and the Division of Diversity and Community Engagement. The financial partnerships allowed us to focus more on our creative goals and less on the financial aspect of publication, but they also led us to question *how these partnerships (in)directly affect what we publish.*

The impact of the financial ties of our partnerships, even with supportive departments or organizations, are important to consider. These stakeholders may potentially impact content, which could be an issue for publications connected to sex(uality) and identity. Our affiliations with university partners made us more cautious and think more thoroughly about any repercussions a student could face for publishing a piece on sex—graphic or otherwise. We also considered the repercussions we could face in terms of funding. "There were so many interwoven questions that you might not have to consider if you're just the poet writing," said Michael. "When I'm writing for myself, I'm like, yeah, screw that, I can write what I want to write, but when your art is positioned within the context of financial relationships or organizational authority, it changes things."

Paul Feigenbaum and Veronica House argue even the most thoughtful partnerships can lead to unintended negative consequences. They suggest community literacy projects interrogate the ways "power imbalances and implicit biases manifest in the relationships" and face the "implications of austerity capitalism" (2). Financial support can help sustain publications, but it may not be worth committing to a university partnership if the organization wants to exert any editorial control. It's important to have discussions about these issues with potential partners so the publication can maintain its creative freedom and speak to the community it hopes to help represent. Ultimately, our university partners didn't ask to have any input on our content. They wanted to help us reach our goals and celebrate the work. Also, when we shifted to a digital publication, we didn't need nearly as much financial support as initially projected, so digital-only publications may be a good option for others in a similar position.

Community Networks

In fall 2021, we organized a release party on campus in the LGBTQ+ lounge—a dedicated space for queer students and faculty in a campus classroom building. One of the publication's exigencies was to help create community networks, and we thought a release party would be a fun and social way to further make these connections. We also wanted to celebrate the great art and writing from the contributors as well as honor the hard work the editorial team had put into the issue over the course of nearly two years.

We invited three *Missy* contributors and one out faculty member to read their work. Because of COVID-19, this was one of the first times we'd been able to mask up and gather in a physical space together. One of the readers joked that he hadn't been around this many queer people in a while, and that he'd "forgotten how to be gay." Another reader came out to the crowd as trans and gave a moving reading of their work.

During intermission, a student performed a duet with his teacher; he played the saxophone while she played the flute. A *Missy* editor had insisted there be live music at this event, so she messaged the university's music department and made it happen.

After intermission, we hosted an open mic so other community members who felt compelled to read their work could participate. Over fifty people attended the event, and an attendee commented on how the event's energy was electric and positive. We had submissions and an editor application emailed to us by the next week.

Conclusion

Missy started as an idea by one student who wanted to increase LGBTQ+ visibility on campus. I became part of this community literacy project because of my visibility as an out professor on a conservative campus. A team of student editors then worked to create networks of community voices through this text. Jason Luther, Frank Farmer, and Stephen Parks argue in community literacy contexts "voice is real because it is originally social, not individual" and these "voices are heard, and only heard, because they exist in relation to other voices" (1). We hoped the zine would create a counter-public for LGBTQ+ voices, but we also needed to consider the potential (negative) outcomes of its circulation to other audiences. There are progressive pockets of the Deep South, but some students still feared they'd be disowned by their families for their sexuality or would face repercussions from campus networks. The nature of the queer subjectivity—and the potential for violence to be enacted on these bodies— made us deeply consider our rhetorical ecologies.

Educators who might want to create a similar literacy project or connect youth with such publications must seriously consider localized contexts and the time it can take to produce this kind of work in marginalized communities. Because this was a self-sponsored literacy project, we didn't have a designated class time to meet or deadlines to make. Ultimately, these factors worked in our favor because we had the time to engage in conversations about many complicated issues. "The process helped us build community," said Michael. "It brought together a group of people who would have never otherwise met, and who probably wouldn't have come together in this same way." COVID-19 delayed our production, but it's important to internalize that these types of projects can't be rushed. This kind of work in programs or courses needs adequate time/space with participants to engage in layered conversations of representation.

I'd never worked so closely and for so long with a group of LGBTQ+ students. I enjoyed the process, and my investment in the project made me think about the sustainability of such student-led literacy projects. The student editors were all passionate and brought energy to the project, but this doesn't mean a similar group of students will emerge. Because this project wasn't tied to a class, it might publish intermittently or only last a few issues like some of the queer zines that came before it. I hope this project continues to provide LGBTQ+ students a space for self-expression, but I don't want to put too much pressure on its future. We're here and queer *now*, and *Missy* is helping the UM campus get more used to it.

Works Cited

Campbell, Ellie. "A Week in the Life of Ole Miss: February 2019 and the Fight to Take Down the Confederate Statue." *The Activist Review*, 16 Dec. 2019, https://activisthistory.com/2019/12/16/a-week-in-the-life-of-ole-miss-february-2019-and-the-fight-to-take-down-the-confederate-statue/. Accessed Nov. 2021.

Duncombe, Stephen. *Notes from Underground: Zines and the Politics of Alternative Culture.* Verso, 1997.

Feigenbaum, Paul, and Veronica House. "The Promising and Challenging Present of Community Literacy." *Community Literacy Journal*, vol. 12, no. 2, 2018, pp. 1-4.

Fraser, Nancy. "Rethinking the Public Sphere: A Contribution to the Critique of Actually Existing Democracy." *Social Text*, vol. 25-26, no. 25/26, 1990, pp. 56-80.

Luther, Jason, et al. "The Past, Present, and Future of Self- Publishing: Voices, Genres, Publics." *Community Literacy Journal*, vol. 12, no. 1, 2017, p. 2.

Martella, Michael, panelist. Panel discussion. Identity Across the Curriculum Conference, 18 March, 2021, University of Mississippi, Oxford, MS.

Missy. "Call for Submissions." January 2020.

Obear, Kathy. "Homophobia." *Beyond Tolerance: Gays, Lesbians, and Bisexuals on Campus*, edited by Nancy Evans and Vernon Wall. American College Personnel Association, 1991, pp. 39-66.

Opperman, Megan. "Intentionally Public, Intentionally Private: Gender Non-Binary Youth on Tumblr and the Queering of Community Literacy Research." *Community Literacy Journal*, vol. 12, no. 2, 2018, pp. 65-71.

Quint, Chella. *Activism Through Zines.* 2013. *Queer Zine Archive Project*, https://archive.qzap.org/index.php/Detail/Object/Show/object_id/425. Accessed Nov. 2021.

Warner, Michael. "Publics and Counterpublics." *Public Culture*, vol. 14, no. 1, 2002, pp. 49-90.

Author Bio

Tyler Gillespie is a doctoral candidate in the English: Writing, Rhetoric, and Technical Communication program at the University of Memphis. He's the author of *Florida Man: Poems* and the essay collection *The Thing about Florida: Exploring a Misunderstood State.*

Payment in the Polity: Funded Community Writing Projects

Audrey Simango, Matthew Stadler, and Alison Turner

Abstract

In this collaborative essay Audrey Simango, Matthew Stadler, and Alison Turner—Reader/Advisor/Editors (RAEs) at The GOAT PoL—explore the subject of money. Most discussions about money have focused on "debates over compensation" of research subjects (Snow et al. 54), or connections between community writing and well-funded projects, such as the Federal Writers Project of the 1930s (Mutnick). After providing context for The GOAT PoL, we reflect on the way our small payments to participants shift our relationships. We ask: 1) How does the exchange of money on The GOAT PoL affect the RAE's experience of reading, editing, and advising authors? 2) How do the challenges we encounter by paying authors make visible what we thought we knew about power and privilege across international writing projects?; and 3) Is it possible for the exchange of money—with its unpredictable impacts—to expand and deepen, rather than shrink and diminish, the polity of literature?

Keywords: community writing, funding, international community writing, polity of literature

In most community writing projects participants are not paid for their writing. The facilitator, workshop leader, or writing consultant might be offered a stipend—or a line on their CV, if they are in academia; but the people who show up to write or submit usually participate voluntarily, to get the experience or further opportunities. On the other hand, in most commercial publishing platforms based on submissions, the publisher selects a few pieces while rejecting scores more, and then makes money by selling the work in the market, sharing some of the profit—when there is profit—with the writer. Often publishers will charge all of the writers who apply to be published ten or twenty dollars for the privilege of applying. Our community writing project takes the relationship between author and publisher and flips it upside-down. At The GOAT PoL (The Geopolitical Open Atlas of The Polity of Literature), we publish every writer who asks, and we pay every writer who chooses to work with us 60 euros. Funded by a Canadian arts foundation, the Musagetes Foundation, with payments originating in Guelph, Ontario, Canada, The GOAT PoL also supports a team of six Reader/Advisor/Editors (RAEs, pronounced "ray"), located in Zimbabwe, Spain, Germany, the United States, and the Netherlands. RAEs are paid a monthly stipend of 400 euros to read, advise, and edit the work of any writer who submits to The GOAT PoL. Our goal is to help authors complete their work and publish it on our site.[1] Publishing on our site is non-exclusive, meaning writers can publish the same piece elsewhere, if they wish. There is no limit on the number of times a writer can submit and publish on The GOAT PoL.

In this collaborative essay three RAEs from The GOAT PoL—Audrey Simango, Matthew Stadler, and Alison Turner—explore a topic that we can't seem to simplify: money. We attempt to loosen the knot that complicates our work as RAEs in this project, and, we presume, the work that takes place in other funded community-writing projects. We hope that this essay brings attention to the relatively quiet published dialog around money and community writing, most of which focuses on the "debates over compensation" of research subjects in settings of complex power dynamics (Snow et al. 54), or connections between community writing and large-scale funded projects, such as the Federal Writers Project of the 1930s (Mutnick). Here, after providing a brief context for The GOAT PoL, we reflect on how small payments to individual participants affects the work of community writing. We group our guiding questions into three categories: 1) How does the exchange of money on The GOAT PoL affect a RAE's experience of reading, editing, and advising authors?; 2) How do the challenges that we encounter when trying to pay authors on The GOAT PoL make visible or nuance what we thought we knew about power and privilege across international community writing projects?; and 3) Is it possible that the exchange of money—with its inevitable though mostly undesired impact on our work with writers—can expand and deepen, rather than shrink and diminish, the polity of literature?

What is a polity of literature?

The GOAT PoL aims to create a living polity of literature in which we write, read, and work together. In this project, a polity is the collective "space of appearance" that Hannah Arendt refers to in her analysis of Aristotle's *On Politics*. In *The Human Condition*, Arendt writes, "The *polis*, properly speaking, is not the city-state in its physical location; it is the organization of the people as it arises out of acting and speaking together for this purpose, no matter where they happen to be...It is the space of appearance in the widest sense of the word, namely, the space where I appear to others as others appear to me" (198-9). Following Aristotle, Arendt understood "politics" as the human capacity for action and expression that arises in each of us whenever we gather as equals in a "space of appearance." Our agency, belonging, and collective potential is catalyzed by this uniquely human arrangement.

A polity of literature happens when such a space manifests as writing-and-reading together—that is, in the shared space of texts that we write or read, wherein we can encounter and witness one another as equals. We choose the term "literature" to describe this uniquely potent space of writing-and-reading together because we understand literature to be essentially different from other sorts of writing-and-reading. In The GOAT PoL's founding essay, "Potatoes or Rice?", an anonymous author explains:

> By 'literature' [we] mean that writing for which every reader has equal authority to make its meanings . . .. Literature proves nothing. It asks us to judge for ourselves . . .. Literature opens a space of appearance in which we become equals, needing no defense. This contentious plurality, the vivid cacophony of contradictory readings in a polity of literature, is where [we] find [our] agency and belonging.

Normally, writers find their readers in the marketplace by selling what they make to a buyer, an intermediary called "the publisher". Not so here: The GOAT PoL is a polity and not a marketplace.

In The GOAT PoL, we accept and work on any writing that isn't generated by an AI chat-bot that's sent to us by any writer who isn't plagiarizing. Those who submit writing might want to work on three sentences or ten pages; they might have never shown their work to anyone, or they might be widely published; they might not call themselves "writers" at all; they might submit one thing and never return, or always have something "churning in the PoL"; they might be stateless with no legal ID, or imprisoned, or living in a refugee camp; they might be displaced, unhoused, or they might have comfortable homes and well-paying professional careers. We can never predict who we'll be working with next when we "claim" new stories from the daily email that shows us new submissions. A writer works with a RAE until both author and RAE believe the story is "ready to publish"; when we publish the story the writer receives sixty euros. Audrey, who is a professional journalist in Zimbabwe, points out that sixty euros isn't enough payment for most of the professional writers she knows. It's a low wage. (RAEs are also paid at a less-than full-time wage.) Across the board, The GOAT PoL offers money to everyone who works, but it cannot offer *equitable* payment. This same sixty euros carries a range of economic impacts, depending on each author's circumstances. Some GOAT PoL authors already enjoy economic stability. Two recently sent us stories about using their own economic stability to support other people in their community. Kimberly Mutandiro's "The Difficulties of Homelessness in Johannesburg" and Carmen Fong's "Free99Fridge" both explore how the author responds to her own privileges and comforts when confronted with the hardships around her: urban homelessness in Johannesburg and food insecurity in Atlanta, respectively.

For some of our writers, sixty euros can solve more acute and urgent needs. Many of them live in refugee camps, where the options for employment or financial security are limited, if they exist at all. See, for example, a post by the writer who goes by Emmanuel, "Facing Today, Looking Forward to Tomorrow," in which he describes where he lives:

> Dzaleka refugee camp is very small, congested and surrounded by local villages. This means that refugees lack access to agricultural land as well as the urban economy. As a result most refugees rely entirely on food aid and other external assistance. In the camp, there are individuals who were qualified doctors, engineers, and architects in their home countries. Here, they are forced to depend on others.

For people who are bureaucratically or physically prevented from earning a wage, The GOAT PoL might provide one of their only opportunities to be compensated for their independent labor and ideas. Money is thus a component of The GOAT PoL but not a criterion for working with us. We pay everyone in order to assert the equality of everyone who works, not to redress the injustices of the global economy.

There's no math for calculating the value of what is exchanged when writers share their work with readers. This is especially true in that strange, vulnerable stage when the reader acts as an advisor or editor. When a writer has germinated a new text, the necessary next step is to enlist a trusted reader to read it and start a conversation about the writing. This collective space of writing and reading is precisely what The GOAT PoL addresses. We bring thoughtful and experienced attention to the writer's work at a vulnerable juncture, when the writer knows *that* they have written, but does not yet know *what* they have written.

Most of the time, this process is delightful. As RAEs, all of us have encountered serious writers, who push us as editors to the edge. These are the writers who make follow-ups on their edits, the writers who want to know what can be done to make their work more ambitious, more developed and evolving, like fine wine. These writers come to The GOAT PoL with energy. One example is Nolleen Mhonda, author of "I can't drive to America, but hell, I'll write of it," who wanted his RAE, Audrey, to know the reasons behind every edit and punctuation that he proposed. Such writers are a daily reminder that writers and editors can establish engaged and thorough-going interactions that can continue. If properly fueled, passion for writing can act as a driving force between the writer and editor during the process of working together and toward the product that others can read afterward.

The process of reading, advising, and editing is not transactional. And yet we simultaneously insist on paying authors for this meaningful exchange. The exchange we initiate by soliciting the work of writers—and promising to honor it with both readerly/advisory/editorial attention *and* a paycheck—creates a double-bind. The exchanges are unalike. On the one hand we promise to show up as RAEs. And on the other, we promise to pay the writer. The two promises are so dissimilar that we have tried in many ways to separate them—tried, and, ultimately, failed.

I. Payment Tainting the Polity?

By choosing to pay all of our writers, The GOAT PoL puts the troublesome process of payment right in the middle of the already delicate process of reading and editing. Matthew, who conceived of and planned this project, prefers to separate the work of Reading/Advising/Editing from the process of paying the writers. He asked the foundation's accountant to deal with all payments, so that RAEs could say to writers, "as RAE and writer, our relationship is only about writing, not money; if there's a problem with money, please speak to the accountant." But some writers make it clear that if we work with them on their writing we are expected to help solve the problems of payment that follow. This begins when questions like "When should I expect my first payment?" start to displace our energetic dialogues about punctuation, metaphors, and audience.

For Audrey, when an interaction between RAE/writer becomes money-focused, it begins to feel like her other work as a professional journalist. As an editor and a RAE, Audrey hopes that the days between claiming a new piece to work on and publishing it will be more of a journey than a process. But when there's money in sight, most writers do not have this view. At times, writers can be so money-oriented that when receiving final edits for an article, they can blatantly tell you to go ahead with all edits and notify them when the payment goes through. What could have been a beautiful journey full of reflection and conversations about literature is turned into a rushed process for payment. This is what can happen when a writer submitting to The GOAT PoL thinks "I need quick cash and l need it fast" rather than "I want to expand my literary horizons. I want to live and breathe writing."

Knowing that an author is edgy for payment can change how we read, advise, and edit. It becomes difficult for the RAE to do their work thoroughly if the writer is in a hurry to get paid. If we don't respond immediately—or quickly enough for them—these writers might get agitated, pressuring us to sacrifice quality for speed. If we are passionate about what we do, this can have a toll that is emotional as well as physical. When pressured to skip over *all that RAE-writer relationship babble* and hit "publish," we might feel a bit scammed: is this writer in it only for the money? But a writer scamming The GOAT PoL is dubious. It's too poor of a payoff. And even if they mean to scam us, can't we insist on writing and revision and all the work that goes with it, before agreeing to publish? And if we do that—if the RAE insists on more work before publishing—is it possible that the writer might feel that *we* are trying to scam *them*?

We might ask ourselves as RAEs what we do when payment for work we have done is delayed. Imagine spending time on a story with a RAE, having accepted the deal of entering the polity—a deal that also promises sixty euros—and then not receiving payment soon after finishing your story. Imagine your RAE doesn't respond for three days after you have worked hard on revisions. Would you perhaps think that this whole thing was a joke? That this magical website that pays you for writing was just…a scam?

II. Power and Privilege in the Polity

Many authors reach out to RAEs about payment because sometimes payments *are* delayed, caught up in the virtual, international knot of wire transfers and online payments. Further, there is no one else to whom they can reach out. If The GOAT PoL payment is going to take a writer through the next day or week, don't they have every right to insist on a timely payment? Can we really blame these writers for asking about their payments? It is work, right? Isn't that what we told them when we promised we'd pay them?

But we didn't think we were paying them in a per-story exchange; we thought we were paying authors to engage in the polity of literature. Perhaps we have rosy-colored classes as RAEs who are compensated on a monthly stipend, rather than a per-story basis. As RAEs, we have the privilege to engage the polity with slowness. If we look at this cynically, it actually behooves us to take as long as we can with each author, since no matter how many authors we work with each month, we receive the same stipend. Should we perhaps ask ourselves: would we behave differently as RAEs if we were paid by each story published, rather than through one payment at the end of each month? While RAEs have the power to publish an author's story, we also have the privilege of imposing slowness when we wish to.

While we knew when the project began that payment would not be a smooth process for every author on The GOAT PoL, we did not anticipate the degree to which we now work with authors on a nuanced and individual basis to ensure that they receive their payment. Initially, we offered authors three payment options: a bank wire transfer, PayPal, or Western Union. An author would work with a RAE, the RAE would hit *publish*, and then the accountant at Musagetes would send the author sixty euros. However, we found that most of our writers don't have bank accounts, and thus don't have PayPal either. And many cannot use Western Union for various reasons. So, working with the accountant at Musagetes, Diana Hillier, we added options for MoneyGram and World Remit, two platforms designed for the international movement of small amounts of money. All of these platforms come with their own set of frustrations, fees, and quirks—the accountant has several times needed to call Western Union for an *interview* in which she explains that this is not—and here's that word again—"a scam."

In addition to all the complications discussed above, there are also unpredictable, inconsistent, and substantial transfer fees. The fees are often subtracted from what the author receives when trying to collect their sixty euros. That is, if the writer can fetch the fee on her own. One author told us she had to hire a "businessman" to collect the money for her. She wrote, "The businessman charged $10 per $100 to $500. This is the same as paying for transport when you withdraw money from a nearby town." How far do we take our promise to work with authors and pay them sixty euros? Is part of our promise that authors receive the full sixty-euro payment, regardless of the layers of fees and disadvantages that might intervene? Does our promise mean we should do the extra work to make sure that the fee for every form of "businessman" (whether it is a virtual transfer fee or a person who takes a bus into town) is also compensated? Is it our job to make sure authors get their equal payment, regardless of the circumstances in which they live, which may or may not determine how they can access funds?

And what does any of this have to do with a polity of literature?

III. Payments as Part of the Polity?

Our writers use a great range of different technologies to write and send us their writing. Some writers have personal laptops and are savvy with spellcheck technology; others do their writing on smartphones or iPads, or at community Internet centers. Some writers need to wait hours or days to find a wifi signal needed for accessing our site and email. There's a similarly wide range of differences in the experiences our writers have when trying to collect their payments.

It is the writers, as much as the RAEs, who are innovating responses to these differences. Sometimes our writers voluntarily collect payment on the behalf of others, as a way to help out without needing "businessmen." And there are many other ways that authors are responding, making new relationships and processes that expand the range and "substance" of our polity. Although it arises from the unintended hardships of receiving payment, there is something lovely about the polity extending itself this way beyond the story posted on the site.

For example, Stephen Pech Gai, a writer from South Sudan who lives in Zimbabwe, has no bank account. He can't use a bank transfer or PayPal. In the decade that he's been fleeing from sectarian violence in his home country, he lived for five years in Kenya, where he was granted refugee status, but was then lured to Zimbabwe for a college education, only to endure much suffering that included the loss of academic opportunity. Zimbabwe has taken more than five years to determine his refugee status application, so he has no state ID. That means he's also been barred from using Western Union, MoneyGram, or World Remit. To pay Stephen for the poems and stories he writes, he asks us to send sixty euros by Western Union to his friend in the camp, a woman Stephen trusts, and she collects the payment using her state ID. Then she gives the cash to Stephen. Another author in Kakuma refugee camp in Kenya helps his neighbors through a similar process, though he has access through World Remit to receive money on his mobile phone, which he cashes out and passes along to the relevant author. Many authors that we work with combine payments, waiting to publish three stories instead of one before receiving funds to make fewer trips to town, and/or they combine payments with one another, hoping to decrease their fees.

As we try to escape the marketplace that obstructs so many writers from reaching audiences, we simultaneously create a system that insists on paying authors—and RAEs—for their reading and writing. The irony of bringing payment into the polity will never go away, no matter how focused we stay on our own practices of reading, advising, and editing. Perhaps, just like RAEs, writers, too, wish that they could say "please speak to the accountant" when it comes to money. Perhaps all of us, RAEs and writers, wish that we could focus only on writing and reading. And yet even as we are forced to think, worry about, and attend to matters of money, a typical day in The GOAT PoL involves writers from across the globe writing and sharing their stories with the RAEs, first of all, and, after publication, with an unknown number of strangers who find the story on our map. Even as their writing tells us more about their lives, the one constant is that what they've experienced is largely unknown to us. Similarly, we cannot fully understand what the payment means to each individual writer, nor can we ignore that this payment affects their relationship to The GOAT PoL, if not their relationship with us. A typical day for a writer on The GOAT PoL might include excitement about payment, but we can only imagine it must always be about something else, too: that precise feeling that comes when we've shared with others what we know to be important.

Notes

1. There are many other components of The GOAT PoL that readers of *Community Literacy Journal* might find compelling. For example, there is no "house style," so that a RAE works with a writer independently from any other writer/RAE relationship. We also publish pieces in infinite "Englishes," supporting an author's language as it operates in their contexts. To learn more about the origins and spirit behind this project, see Matthew Stadler's essay "Goat Literature: A Future PoL" and visit the site at https://thegoatpol.org.

Works Cited

Anonymous, "Potatoes or Rice?" *artseverywhere*, Mar. 12, 2020. https://www.artseverywhere.ca/the-polity-of-literature-potatoes-or-rice/. Accessed 25 Jan. 2023.

Arendt, Hannah. *The Human Condition*, introduction by Margaret Canovan, 2nd edition, U of Chicago P, 1998.

Emmanuel. "Facing Today, Looking Forward to Tomorrow." *The GOAT PoL*, 19 Nov. 2022, https://thegoatpol.org/story/facing-today-looking-forward-to-tomorrow/. Accessed 25 Jan. 2023.

Fong, Carmen. "Free99Fridge." *The GOAT PoL*, 21 Oct. 2022, https://thegoatpol.org/story/free99fridge/. Accessed 25 Jan. 2023.

Mhonda, Nolleen. "I can't drive to America, but hell, I'll write of it." *The GOAT PoL*, 26 Oct. 2022, https://thegoatpol.org/story/i-cant-drive-to-america-but-hell-ill-write-of-it/. Accessed 25 Jan. 2023.

Mutandiro, Kimberly. "The Difficulties of Homelessness in Johannesburg," *The GOAT PoL*, 25 Nov. 2022. https://thegoatpol.org/story/the-difficult-lives-of-homeless-people-in-johannesburg/. Accessed 25 Jan. 2023.

Mutnick, Deborah. "Write. Persist. Struggle: Sponsors of Writing and Workers' Education in the 1930s." *Community Literacy Journal*, vol. 11, no. 1, 2016, pp. 10–21, doi:10.25148/clj.11.1.009245.

Snow, Rachel C., et al. "Paying to Listen: Notes from a Survey of Sexual Commerce." *Community Literacy Journal*, vol. 8, no. 1, 2013, pp. 53–69, doi:10.25148/clj.8.1.009329.

Stadler, Matthew. "Goat Literature: A Future PoL." *artseverywhere*, 2022. https://www.artseverywhere.ca/goat-literature/. Accessed 25 Jan. 2023.

Author Bios

Audrey Simango is a freelance food journalist who joined The GOAT PoL as a RAE in August 2022. She has worked with several publishers and her journalism reports have been online published in *Remedy Health Media* (Thebody.com USA), *New Internationalist* (England), and *The South Africa.com* (South Africa), *Newsweek* magazine, *The Africa Report* (Paris), and *iAfrikan News*. She is also a food engineer, currently based in Zimbabwe.

Matthew Stadler is a writer and editor, the author of the novels *Allan Stein, Landscape: Memory, The Dissolution of Nicholas Dee,* and *The Sex Offender.* He is the recipient of Guggenheim and Ingram-Merrill fellowships, a Whiting Writer's Award, and a United States Artists fellowship. He edits the Fellow Travelers Series of books and is the founder and a Reader/Advisor/Editor at The GOAT PoL. He lives in Rotterdam and Seattle.

Alison Turner has been a RAE with The GOAT PoL since the summer of 2022. She is a member of the editorial collective for Coda, the creative section in *Community Literacy Journal,* and has a collection of short stories forthcoming with Torrey House Press. She is an ACLS Leading Edge postdoctoral fellow at Operation Shoestring in Jackson, Mississippi, where she is working on a community-based oral history project.

Access as Praxis: Navigating Spaces of Community Literacy in Graduate School

Millie Hizer

Abstract

In this article, I reflect on my lived experiences as a disabled graduate student navigating spaces of community literacy. This essay utilizes storytelling as an entry point for understanding the barriers graduate students oftentimes face while accessing community literacy projects. Extending Ada Hubrig's theorization of *disability justice informed community literacy,* I propose an "access as praxis" approach to community literacy projects that listens to the access needs of graduate students looking to form meaningful relationships with community partners.

Keywords: accessibility, disability justice, graduate school, lived experience, praxis

I left the virtual conference space at the 2021 Conference on Community writing with a renewed vigor for community literacy studies. After attending multiple panels, round tables, and deep think tanks that provided a glimpse into the power of community literacy initiatives, I once again found myself eagerly wanting to embody the role of a community engaged scholar.

However, doing this type of meaningful work has at times seemed beyond my grasp. As a disabled, neurodivergent scholar, my body-mind is easily overwhelmed—I must carefully decide how to distribute my labor. Even though I want to be more involved in community engaged work, I know that my success in academia depends on my ability to fit the narrow confines of a neoliberal university system. Within this system, I'm an expendable, disabled graduate student whose labor is situated "against a backdrop of ableist structures" ("On Crip Doulas"). Working within a system that fails to prioritize socially conscious work in the service of productivity and capitalist ventures has meant that my commitment to social justice initiatives has fallen by the wayside.

In this essay, I will work alongside scholarship that values storytelling and life writing as valuable research methodologies. I agree with Christina Cedillo's formulation of life writing as "a method for re-presenting events and experiences from the viewpoints of oppressed people in order to challenge narratives composed from the standpoint of the privileged perspective" ("What does it Mean to Move?"). While my own perspective is admittedly limited, I will utilize my lived experiences as a framework for *beginning* to understand how both graduate student labor conditions and a lack of institutional support can serve as significant barriers for disabled graduate students looking to engage in community literacy projects. Ultimately, I will suggest what I call an "access as praxis" approach towards community literacy. Extending Ada Hubrig's orientation to the field in "'We Move Together:' Reckoning With Disability Justice in Community Literacy Studies," an access as praxis approach begins by looking at community literacy studies through a Disability Justice lens. Invoking Sins Invalid's principle of *collective access*, an access as praxis methodology means exploring "ways of doing things that go beyond able-bodied and neurotypical norms" (13). It brings visibility to the barriers preventing disabled graduate students from meaningfully engaging in community engaged work.

Barriers Towards Access

The *work* of community literacy (see Kynard, 2019) is oftentimes contingent on unpredictable circumstances; this is a risk many graduate students on strict graduation timelines cannot afford to take. In a 2017 report detailing Graduate Student Instructor Labor Conditions in Writing Programs, 71.6% of graduate student instructors (GSIs) interviewed admitted that their student stipends failed to cover their living expenses. Ultimately, the report concludes that "The labor conditions of GSIs are woefully inadequate" (Osorio et al.). It is no wonder that participating in unpaid community literacy work isn't feasible for many graduate students.

Furthermore, community literacy work can at times be overlooked as a valuable cite for scholarly knowledge production. For instance, in a 2014 case study detailing a graduate level community literacy seminar, the authors express concern that the field "remains at the fringes of the academy," which discourages graduate students from participating in community engaged projects (Bowen et al.). While graduate programs have begun to recognize the value of community partnerships over recent decades, more attention needs to be paid to the accessibility of those partnerships.

This sentiment highlights the difficulty many graduate students face when attempting to do community engaged work. This is further complicated when disability becomes a factor. A recent report from The National Institute on Disability indicates that "Working-age adults with disabilities are twice as likely as those without disabilities to have incomes under the poverty threshold" (Goodman et al. 2). This is the grim reality so many disabled graduate students face. For graduate students working for near poverty wages, any additional labor must be carefully negotiated. Therefore, engaging in community engaged scholarship that may or may not be valued by graduate departments and hiring committees can be especially inaccessible for disabled scholars. In an increasingly competitive academic market, it is no secret that one must be strategic in choosing opportunities. So, when certain types of scholarship are privileged over others, it means that many graduate students must carefully navigate these intricacies in order to be successful in their careers, even if it means foregoing their passions for more traditionally "practical" work.

Disabled graduate students must also always consider the fact that their health could decline at any moment. With COVID-19 as a pivotal concern, disabled graduate students are at an even greater risk when participating in community partnerships that typically occur in-person. In turn, it is crucial to acknowledge that disabled graduate students need more institutional support—not only to engage in community literacy projects, but to live. More specifically, the field needs to interrogate why in-person engagement is oftentimes prioritized and how graduate programs can more fully support students interested in remote community literacy work. For multiply marginalized scholars, "COVID intensified how the lack of access and support accelerates the physical dangers always already present in our lives" (Hubrig and Cedillo 1). Without access to the supports and protections afforded by more stable employment, engaging in community literacy work can be a risk many graduate students cannot afford to take.

An access as praxis approach begins to address these barriers by placing accessibility at the forefront of community literacy studies. This means seeing the field through a lens of Disability Justice. As Ada Hubrig continues in "We Move Together," a "disability justice informed community literacy" looks "to create new partnerships that might dismantle the power structures that threaten disabled people and other marginalized communities" (150). However, in order to do so, these relationships need to be accessible for all involved. For Hubrig and Cedillo, in "Access as Community Literacy," "Accessibility should be centered in the creation and maintaining of intersectional and interdependent praxes with careful attention to who is being asked to shoulder the labor of access" (4). Put simply, the labor of access should be a collective enterprise—one that is not solely shouldered by the disabled community or graduate students themselves.

My Story

I began my graduate school journey with community literacy engagement in the Spring of 2019 when I took a service-learning course. After completing the required training, I began working as an English Language tutor at the Volunteers in Tutoring Adult Learners (VITAL) program in my community. Essentially, VITAL is a tutoring program run through the Bloomington, Indiana, public library that aims to improve the literacy skills of adult learners in our community. Here, there are options to tutor learners in basic literacy skills, English as a Second Language (ESL), and computer literacy skills. When I was paired with my tutee, an ESL student whose primary goal was to improve her English literacy skills, I immediately told her that I was tutoring at VITAL as part of a service-learning course at my university. At first, I wasn't sure how long I'd be able to work with the program but wanted to continue as long as I could. However, once my tutee decided to leave Bloomington, it was difficult to find the motivation to continue with the program.

As someone diagnosed with both obsessive compulsive disorder (OCD) and attention-deficit hyperactivity disorder (ADHD), I tend to overcommit to projects while simultaneously obsessing over doing those projects "perfectly"—as if there is such a thing. So, it's no wonder that my second year of graduate school I found myself taking a full course-load while working a demanding part-time job, teaching first-year writing, and working as a literacy tutor. Put simply, I had overextended myself and my health began to suffer. Therefore, when my assigned tutee moved away from Bloomington, my commitment to the program dwindled.

Then, the pandemic hit, and the library closed for months. For multiple reasons, I felt lost. I was in a much better place health-wise but didn't feel comfortable tutoring in-person at VITAL. So, I began looking for remote opportunities for community engaged work. Throughout the pandemic, I learned that remote work is more accessible for my neurodivergent mind. At home, I can take medication without judgment; I can process complex information with my emotional support animal by my side. I can easily access a restroom if I feel sick; I can feel safe from trauma-related triggers. To put it another way, this type of environment allows me to thrive.

However, I recognize that I come from a privileged position. While the fear of unexpected, exorbitant disability-related medical bills is always at the forefront of my mind, I have a supportive family and partner. I'm a white, cisgender woman working in academia. Even so, I still live with the constant fear that I will find myself hospitalized again and unable to work. So, I've worked multiple side-jobs throughout graduate school to prepare for the worst-case scenario, even though it wasn't always necessary—motivated by my obsessive-compulsive fears that something *could* happen. For disabled graduate students without a similar support system, this type of outside work can become even more of a necessity, leaving little room for community engaged work.

Of course, working with community partners isn't always an easy task. The ever-changing, tactical nature of such projects can make them incredibly time-consuming and unpredictable energy expenditures (Mathieu 28). As my fellow colleague at Indiana University notes, "The risks involved with balancing academic requirements while also maintaining ethically responsible relationships with community partners can be seen as a burden not all graduate students can afford to bear" (McCool 141). Unfortunately, disabled graduate students from multiply marginalized communities are at a greater risk of not being able to maintain sustainable relationships with community partners; if our health suffers, so too can our commitments.

Indeed, there is a certain level of irony in publishing about community literacy work; community engaged researchers are consistently engaged in reciprocal relationships with their community partners. In doing this type of work, I've begun to find a way to merge my own personal and scholarly commitments. However, I'm still searching—I know that I want to become more involved in disability advocacy and community literacy initiatives, but it can be difficult to know where to begin outside of a structured classroom context. Will I be able to find more remote opportunities? Will these opportunities be accessible and flexible? These questions are constantly at the forefront of my mind. I want to do more, but I'm still deciphering what that looks like and how I can still prioritize my own health and wellbeing in the process.

Implementing an Access as Praxis Approach

While there are no easy solutions to the inaccessibility of community literacy work for graduate student instructors, I'd like to propose a potential way forward, which

I will call "access as praxis." Taking inspiration from Cushman's thoughts regarding "The Access in Praxis" I argue that an access as praxis approach can begin to make community literacy projects more accessible for graduate students from multiply marginalized communities (18). For a myriad of reasons, community literacy initiatives that are only accessible to able-bodied, cisgender, heteronormative activists can isolate community partners. Since the pandemic began, digital literacy programs have become even more prolific; such programs could provide disabled graduate students with a more accessible, digital an entry point into the field of community literacy studies. However, the goal is not to limit who can and should engage in community literacy initiatives; rather, it is to acknowledge that community literacy studies needs to be accessible to a variety of bodyminds.

I would therefore like to provide two, short suggestions the field of community literacy studies can take to promote graduate students' access to the field:

1. Support Community Engaged Partnerships in Digital Spaces

Graduate programs that support remote, accessible engagement with community partners will give more disabled and multiply marginalized graduate students the opportunity to engage in community literacy work. If universities continue to support graduate student access needs post-pandemic, especially in terms of allocating funds for assistive technology and access to remote engagement platforms such as Zoom, more disabled graduate students will be able to forge lasting connections with their community partners. For instance, project-based service-learning courses could introduce graduate students to community partnerships that take place in digital spaces. Graduate programs that support remote, accessible engagement with community partners will give more disabled and multiply marginalized graduate students the opportunity to engage in community literacy work that can be more readily sustained.

2. Provide Collective Support for Graduate Students Navigating Community Literacy

The labor of accessibility is oftentimes placed on disabled individuals themselves. This labor corresponds to Anika Konrad's concept of "Access Fatigue" in which "seeking access necessitates that disabled people constantly toggle between self-invention and self-preservation" (180). Within spaces of community literacy, graduate students are typically tasked with finding their own community partnerships that may or may not be able to accommodate their access needs. An access as praxis approach would implement a more robust support system for graduate students looking to engage in community partnerships. This could include the collaborative creation of a structured database listing the different modalities offered for specific community partnerships and additional departmental funding for digital tools that support remote community engagement.

Moving Forward

An access as praxis approach is far from perfect. It also requires change to occur at an institutional level, especially in terms of valuing remote engagement. In truth, I still have more questions than answers. While this piece primarily focuses on graduate student access, it is only a small component of what it means to access community literacy. As Cana Itchuaqiyaq et al. explain, "The concept of access risks misuse; it is all too easy to use the value of 'access' to justify injustices, if access is treated as a universal and unexamined good" (95). To put it another way, accessing spaces of community literacy does not beget a one size fits all approach.

Undoubtedly, there are some community partners who might prefer in-person engagement. An access as *praxis* approach recognizes that the needs of community partners can vary drastically. This approach is not meant to alienate graduate students or community partners who find in-person engagement more accessible; rather, it is to cultivate a dialogue about what constitutes access. One answer could be to encourage graduate students to discuss issues of access with community partners from the start. If a community partner is unable to participate in a project remotely, but would like to, it could be productive to discuss what barrier—such as a lack of infrastructure or technology—are preventing them from doing so. Even so, this isn't a perfect solution. As Hubrig and Cedillo further, "For those doing community literacy work adjacent to university or collegiate power structures—access and lack of access–frequently replicate the same white supremacist, cisheteropatriachal, ableist normativies of institutions" (2-3). This begs the question: How can the field increase access for both graduate students and community partners against a backdrop of inequitable power structures?

With these considerations in mind, I again want to once acknowledge that I come from a privileged position. While the fear of unexpected, exorbitant disability-related medical bills is always at the forefront of my mind, I have a supportive family and partner. I'm a white, cisgender woman working in academia. So, I know that my story cannot fully account for the barriers graduate students face in doing community literacy work. Writing this type of essay also involves navigating some contentious waters. In centering my own story alongside larger considerations of graduate student access, I know that there are pivotal voices that will inevitably be missing from this piece. Namely, this piece has focused on the barriers graduate students face rather than explicitly focusing on community partners themselves. I want to emphasize that this is merely one aspect of accessibility; I do not intend to position graduate students as benevolent saviors rescuing community literacy partners. This would simply reproduce the "colonizing ideology" scholars such as Cushman warn against (11). Instead, this essay simply interrogates one facet of accessibility impacting the complex web of literacy partnerships.

Moving forward, I call for the field of Community Literacy Studies to continue to center accessibility. With the recent publication of *CLJ*'s issue on "Accessing Community Literacies," issues of disability justice, combatting systemic ableism, and promoting a more equitable field that values a multiplicity of bodyminds have been brought to the center of our field. Even so, we can do more. I agree with Hubrig and Cedillo's assertion in their introduction to the special issue—*access* can, and should be seen as "a concept that centers intersectionality, collective responsibility, and community to challenge oppressive logics" (2). Implementing an access as praxis approach is simply one way in which our field can continue to move forward to value and center multiply marginalized voices.

Notes

1. See the Adult Community Learning Services (ACLS) program associated with the Massachusetts Department of Elementary and Secondary Education as an example.

Works Cited

Bowen, Betsy, et al. "Community Engagement in a Graduate-Level Community Literacy Course." *Community Literacy Journal*, vol. 9, no. 1, 2014, pp. 18–38.

Cedillo, Christina V. "What Does It Mean to Move? Race, Disability, and Critical Embodiment Pedagogy." *Composition Forum*, vol. 39, 2018.

Cedillo, Christina V. and Hubrig, Ada. "Access as Community Literacy: A Call for Intersectionality, Reciprocity, and Collective Responsibility." *Community Literacy Journal*, vol. 17, no.1, 2023, pp. 1-8.

Cushman, Ellen. "The Rhetorician as an Agent of Social Change." *College Composition and Communication*, vol. 47, no. 1, 1996, pp. 7–28.

Goodman, Nanette, et al. The Extra Costs of Disability - National Disability Institute. Oct. 2020.

Hubrig, Ada. "On 'Crip Doulas,' Invisible Labor, and Surviving Academia While Disabled." *The Journal of Multimodal Rhetorics,* vol. 5, no. 1, 2021.

---. "'We Move Together:' Reckoning with Disability Justice in Community Literacy Studies." *Community Literacy Journal*, vol. 14, no. 2, 2020, pp. 144-153.

Itchuaqiyaq, Cana, et al. "To Community With Care: Enacting Positive Barriers to Access as Good Relations." *Community Literacy Journal*, vol. 17, no.1, 2023, pp. 94-96.

Konrad, Annika M. "Access Fatigue: The Rhetorical Work of Disability in Everyday Life." *College English*, vol. 83, no. 3, 2021, pp. 179-199.

Kynard, Carmen. "'All I Need is One Mic': A Black Feminist Community Meditation on the Work, the Job, and the Hustle (and Why So Many of Yall Confuse This Stuff)." Conference on Community Writing, 18 Oct. 2019, Irvine Auditorium, University of Pennsylvania. Keynote Address.

Mathieu, Paula. *Tactics of Hope: The Public Turn in English Composition.* Boynton/Cook, 2005.

Massachusetts Department of Elementary and Secondary Education. "ACLS Services." *ACLS Services - Adult and Community Learning Services (ACLS)*, 1 Aug. 2022, https://www.doe.mass.edu/acls/systemci.html.

McCool, Megan. "When Tactical Hope Doesn't Feel Like Enough: A Graduate Student's Reflection on Precarity and Community-Engaged Research." *Community Literacy Journal*, vol. 14, no. 2, 2020, pp. 138-143. doi:10.25148/14.2.009041.

Osorio, Ruth, et al. "Report on Graduate Student Instructor Labor Conditions in Writing Programs," Writing Program Administration Graduate Organization, 2017.

Sins Invalid. *Skin, Tooth, and Bone: The Basis of Movement is Our People*. 2nd ed., digital ed., 2019.

Author Bio

Millie Hizer is a PhD Candidate in Rhetoric and Composition at Indiana University Bloomington where she teaches courses in first-year writing, public speaking, and professional writing. She has published her writing in *enculturation: a journal of rhetoric, writing, and culture*, *The Journal of Multimodal Rhetorics*, and *Spark: A4C4 Equality Journal*. Her work has also been featured on Rhetoric and Writing Studies podcasts such as *Tell me More!* and *Pedagogue*. As a scholar-activist committed to principles of Disability Justice, Millie centers disability storytelling in both her research and pedagogy.

Book and New Media Reviews

From the Book and New Media Review Editor's Desk

Jessica Shumake, Editor
University of Notre Dame

My dissertation advisor and mentor, Ken S. McAllister, taught the students he worked with that scholarly writing is an act of generosity and that the call to write necessitates faith that readers will respect the shared humanity of the writers with whom they engage. When writers imagine ethical and genuinely open encounters with readers, those same writers can also grow to appreciate the chanciness and inherent risk that their words could be interpreted uncharitably. If writers refuse to risk misunderstanding or encounters with disingenuous interlocuters, we foreclose potential communal gathering spaces to share and debate ideas. When readers and writers gather together, these gathering spaces are inherently risky and good faith effort is required to emerge on the other side of the reader-writer encounter with a deeper, changed, or more nuanced understanding.

My role as a witness to good faith encounters between writers and readers is what keeps me serving in an editorial capacity for the *Community Literacy Journal*. The principle of rigorous generosity, which is the journal's "guiding editorial philosophy" renews my faith in the possibility of good relations between writers and their readers (Feigenbaum and House 4). In this issue, I extend sincere thanks to reviewers Walker Smith, Heidi Willers, Lily Deen, Noha Labani, Lauren Piette, Vanessa Sullivan, and Heidi M. Williams and for their perceptive reviews. I hope this section remains consistent in encouraging *CLJ* readers to hear new voices and explore recent books in community writing with a spirit of openness and generosity.

Works Cited

Feigenbaum, Paul, and Veronica House. "The Promising and Challenging Present of Community Literacy." *Community Literacy Journal*, 12.2, 2018, pp. 1–4.

Teaching Through the Archives: Text, Collaboration, and Activism

*Edited by Tarez Samra Graban
and Wendy Hayden*
Southern Illinois University
Press, 2022, 333 pp.

Reviewed by Walker P. Smith
Goucher College

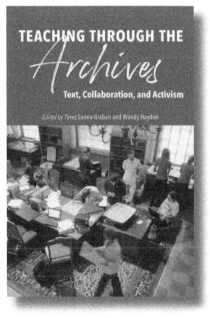

W hen I embarked upon my first research project in a physical archive in 2019, I expected that the
research, and the scholarship that would later
emerge from it, would mostly originate from
the artifacts found within the boxes. Instead,
nearly all of the academic claims I have been
able to make from that collection were the
result of collaborations with archivists, researchers, and community members with in-
vestments in those artifacts. I was well-trained
by archival rhetorics scholarship to perceive the organization of the collection as a
rhetorical act to be studied; however, it was Gesa Kirsch, the professor of our graduate seminar, who modeled for me how to build relationships with the community
in the archives. In the end, these people were primarily the sources who recounted
for me the provenance of the collection: how it originally arrived, how it has evolved
since then, and its relationship with various institutional and community stakeholders. Our conversations, not my physical research, are what led me to locate the items
that spoke to my interests and developed my research questions further.

In Tarez Samra Graban and Wendy Hayden's edited collection *Teaching Through
the Archives: Text, Collaboration, and Activism*, community in the archives is not just
serendipitous but is intentional, fulfilling what Neal Lerner wrote thirteen years ago
in *Working in the Archives* during the rise of rhetoric's archival turn: "archival research
is not merely about the artifacts to be found but is ultimately about the people who
have played a role in creating and using these artifacts" (195–6). Graban and Hayden's
introduction to the collection takes seriously the archive as social process, expanding
from the viewpoint of the researcher to include the students who both learn from and
contribute back to the archives, the community members who have a personal stake
in the artifacts, the institutions that afford or constrain each archival encounter, and
especially the archivists whose labor is valued here not as a "courtesy, but as an integral research methodology for the field" (5). The chapters they selected are intended

to exemplify how they "actively and critically reorient themselves toward *both* the collaboration *and* the archival collection(s)" (5).

This move also highlights what they claim distinguishes rhetoric and composition's archival scholarship from other fields: our "focus on theories of teaching" (5). The questions that guide the collection are: "How do we bring the archives into the classroom? How do students become historians of rhetoric and composition's archives? How do our reflective practices both stem from and contribute to a critical understanding of what to do better?" (5). However, their collection is not limited to the scope of pedagogy but addresses both how we are using archives in our teaching and research while also reflecting on what our patterns of use mean for theory-building about archives in the field. Carving out the archive as a site of "epistemic possibility," the collection serves as more than just an opportunity for "exchanging ideas about teaching or reading in specific archives," which as a reader is already helpful enough on its own, but also forwards a triadic cycle of archival activity that breaks down our work into three interconnected categories: text, collaboration, and activism (14).

These categories divide the collection into its three sections. The 'text' section describes the essays that share "topical inquiry or close/critical reading, and how this approach helps foster the habits of mind that are essential for creating and using archives, for being better stewards of private and public collections, and for making new knowledge practices" (7). The 'collaboration' section features examples of "service learning from the archives" that often lead to "methodological reflection" or "the discovery of shared topics, as we partner with the university archives and archival studies scholars on teaching archival theory and interdisciplinary research" (7, 9). The 'activism' section works "to reveal racial omissions or gender gaps *through* the archives" and features reflections on "the ethical considerations of social justice" (11). The triad, through which all three activities overlap and share "multiple dimensions of the same relationship," presents "an epistemology called *archive*" that may allow for "teaching disruptively with archives" (14, 16).

Part I, 'text,' is work *about* the archives. In this section, authors share assignments that ask students to date unsorted photographs by employing physical context clues in and outside the special collections, assemble timelines of women's history using archival materials, identify and recover women to be included in the rhetorical canon, compose creative nonfiction stories about the people found in the archives, and deconstruct and reassemble once-settled narratives about the history of rhetoric. A key objective of this section is to foreground feminist rhetorics as a foundation for archival scholarship. In chapter one, "Using the Archives to Teach Slow Rhetorics and Create Local Connections," Lisa Mastrangelo challenges her students to trace the "history," "ghost stories," and "traditions" that haunt their (and every) university campus (31). In the process, they must learn "slow research," which is the "slow and careful analysis of documents, the search for information not readily available, and extrapolation of information based on obscure textual clues" (32). As our lives are increasingly marked by hyperattention, the "deep attention" of slow research is both difficult and rewarding for students who find that they research "more effectively" by slowing down and pausing on "patterns and context clues" (32). In chapter two, "Cultivating a

Feminist Consciousness in the University Archive," Lisa Shaver expands Kirsch and Royster's notion of critical imagination from a key archival praxis to a pedagogical exercise, pointing out that the process of critical imagination is often "unspoken and untaught" (48). She offers "inference" as its method, which "requires both evidence and logical reasoning," asking students to connect argument to source by exploring the question, "*What can you logically claim based on this artifact?*" (48).

Part I also asks us to reflect on the student experience of working in archives: What do they learn, feel, and gain from such an assignment? In chapter three, "Arranging Our Emotions: Archival Affects and Emotional Responses," Jane Greer interrogates the pedagogical practice of noting students' emotional reactions to archival materials. We have often relied on their "powerful emotional experiences" as the evidence that our assignments have "impact" or "value" on their learning, but have sometimes failed to interrogate precisely what about the "creation and organization of the archive" has produced "emotional attachments" or "particular affective experiences" (60). Greer performs this mapping in her case study and provides a template for how we can "make space in our classrooms for acknowledging and interrogating" student emotions, as well as connecting them to specific institutional structures (72). In chapter four, "Creative Storytelling: Archives as Sites for Nonfiction Research and Writing," Katherine E. Tirabassi extends the ethical considerations of archival research to other writing workshops. Artifacts provide students with "a resource for creative inspiration, background information, and genre experimentation" while negotiating a shared "code of ethics about creating stories about the past" (76). And in chapter five, "Assembled Trajectories, Perishable Performances, and Teaching from the Harvard Archives," James P. Beasley considers how archival materials might fill gaps in our graduate training. Where traditional approaches have circulated ready-made narratives about the history of rhetorical education that slot certain figures into a "linear development of rhetorical theory," supplementing with tertiary artifacts enabled his seminar students to become active historians who interface with the complex "contingencies of location and institution" that otherwise would have been hidden if they had only read the primary and secondary sources (99, 101).

Part II, 'collaboration,' is work *for* the archives. In this section, authors share assignments that ask students to curate interactive exhibits, preserve project materials for clients and future students, process and evaluate sources about the field of rhetoric and composition, write grant proposals and strategic plans for archivists—*and* that ask instructors to participate in interdisciplinary methods workshops using local collections. In all of these chapters, students and instructors are active contributors to archives themselves. In chapter six, "Internships as *Techne*: Teaching the Archive Through the Museum of Everyday Writing," Jennifer Enoch, et al. employ archiving as an activity where students practice applying keywords in rhetorical theory. *Techne* is the guiding force that informs how students interact with the Museum of Everyday Writing, a digital archive that hosts "texts written by ordinary people in nonacademic and nonprofessional contexts, in order to organize and make sense of their everyday lives and to maintain social relationships" (108). By gaining experience in every aspect of archiving—locating, processing, organizing, tagging, editing, curating, marketing, etc.—they come to understand "how writing shapes day-to-day lives" (108).

In chapter seven, "Listening Rhetorically to Build Collaboration and Community in the Archives," Shirley K Rose, et al. upend the dominant research paradigm that would suggest a researcher should first develop a question and then turn to the archives to seek out the answer. Instead, their students "generate and articulate new research questions in the process of listening to the materials they encounter or that might be placed in front of them" (125). Such an ethics of care is also represented in chapter eight, "Recursion and Responsiveness: Archival Pedagogy and Archival Infrastructures in the Same Conversation," in which Jenna Morton-Aiken and Robert Schwegler flesh out what a relational architecture might mean for conducting archival research. Rather than reproduce the traditional "closed" system in which the user enters, observes, and exits "without having left a trace of work behind," they push for mechanisms like folksonomy hashtags that invite users to "'talk back' in order to record and value multiple ways of knowing and doing," building "web[s]" not "hierarch[ies]" (148, 151).

How knowledge is made, preserved, circulated, and remade is foregrounded in the final two chapters of Part II, which both tailor archival pedagogies to the professional and technical communication classrooms. In chapter nine, "<Ex>tending Archives: Digital Archival Practices and Making the Work of Technical Communicators Visible to Students," Erin Brock Carlson, et al. recast keywords in technical communication that describe document processing—"*content management*, *project management*, and *information infrastructures*"—through the lens of an "archival platform," which they posit as a "metaphor for structuring this intermingling of archival practices with technical communication's management of digital content" (158–9). Archival pedagogy offers the traditional client-based course the "reflexive attention" to not only provide "deliverables" and "accompanying documentation" but also the ability to "locate, use, and adapt resources long after their involvement in the project has ended," which is necessary for building long-term relationships with community partners (168–9). Conversely, in chapter ten, "Professional Writing for the Archives: Collaboration and Service Learning in a Proposal Writing Class," Jonathan Buehl, et al. actually approach the archivist as a client and the special collections as their workspace that requires professional communication. They select archival departments because they see them as "already rich sites" for "experiential learning" through service-learning frameworks and provide opportunities for expanding community literacy through genres like grant proposals (180).

Part III, 'activism,' is work *through* the archives. In this section, authors share assignments that ask students to collect oral histories from community members, write annual reports and feature profiles for community organizations and their initiatives, revise metadata to be more accessible and searchable, deploy archival materials to create and edit Wikipedia articles, recover important civil rights ephemera, reflect on archival silences, and bridge historical and contemporary social movement rhetorics. One objective of this section is to invite students to think more deeply about where they conduct their research and the community members who inhabit those places.

In chapter eleven, "Delinking Student Perspectives of Place With/in the University Archive," Laura Proszak and Ellen Cushman retool the institutional archive as a site for "speaking back to Western or accepted knowledge-making practices" in which "students imagine and reinvent alternatives to representations with archival documents and the communities represented in the archives" (198). Physical archival research is tied to the work of community engagement, connecting their coursework to the "legacies of interactions that preceded their interactions with community members and the university archive" (199, 206). In chapter twelve, "Archives as Resources for Ethical In(ter)vention in Community-Based Writing," Michael-John DePalma finds that such community-based writing projects that employ archives can develop students' "rhetorical humility," which is a "nuanced understanding of how various social forces create the needs that community partners work to address" (213). By more critically linking "archive" and "community," he argues that we can "heighten writers' awareness of ethical considerations and foster writers' ethical dispositions," pushing us to consider the following question in each of our assignments: "What kinds of writers are we inviting our students to become?" (213).

Part III also explores how community-engaged archival work might open up opportunities for students to witness what the editors termed the "epistemology called *archive*" in action (16). In chapter thirteen, "Learning to (Re)Compose Identities: Creating and Indexing the JHFE Jewish Kentucky Oral History Repository with Undergraduate Researchers and Jewish Rhetorical Practices," Janice W. Fernheimer, et al. develop community-informed archival methods that enact the ways of knowing and doing that are embodied in Jewish rhetorics. Such "collaborative epistemic practices" are implemented in how they interviewed, indexed, and interfaced with people and archival materials, which in turn, helps them to revise "their understanding of what knowledge is, how it is produced, and how they participate in its production and presentation" (231–2). In chapter fourteen, "'Flagged for Deletion': Wikipedia, the Federal Writers' Project, and First-Year Composition," Courtney Rivard harnesses students' digital literacy skills by applying archival sources to Wikipedia editing efforts. In doing so, they practice using their research to make "small ruptures in the systems" that uphold "Western epistemologies" and "to directly impact the historical record through digital writing aimed at a public audience," learning from both their successes and their failures (248, 259).

Finally, Part III demonstrates how we can support social movements through our archival pedagogies. In chapter fifteen, "Is Anyone Sitting Here?: Mirroring Gaillet's 'Survival Steps' in a Community-Based, Justice-Focused Classroom," Jeanne Law-Bohannon and Shiloh Gill Garcia model student-instructor partnerships that engage students in activism outside the university; they argue for us to "compose public works together, collaboratively creating texts that have value to communities outside university walls" (263). These alliances aid community organizations, whose work is time-sensitive, while also creating learning opportunities for students to "find, curate, corroborate, and tell the stories of underrepresented groups who have been forgotten or minimized by history" (276). In chapter sixteen, "'Loving Blackness' as a First-Year Composition Student Learning Outcome in the Archives," the core goal of archival pedagogy is "to recognize a local antecedent to contemporary social justice efforts that assert the value of Black lives" (279). Responding to students' tendencies to adopt "the language of outrage that merely *described* violence," Michelle S. Hite, et al. utilize archiving as a contextualizing tool for student research by centering "Black survival as an archival artifact" and "loving blackness" as an "epistemological core" (279, 281). This "expanded vocabulary" enables a research agenda for first-year students to "*contemplate, study*, and *record* Black life through terms meant for its flourishing" (281).

Readers of *Community Literacy Journal* will no doubt find this collection to be an extensive and dynamic resource for designing and implementing archival activities and assignments at a wide range of scales; for harnessing archives and/or archiving in community-engaged courses, and vice versa; and for composing the language necessary to justify the student learning outcomes of an archival pedagogy in rhetoric, composition, and professional and technical writing. The descriptions are accessible and detailed enough for novices to adopt and experiment with in their own classrooms, while also offering experts new ideas, strategies, readings, and concepts to reinvigorate their existing curricula. Importantly, though, the editors are careful to note that the essays, when considered together, further the field's knowledge about what it means to archive. Of course, the authors expand our definitions of many archival rhetorics keywords: critical imagination (chapter two), emotion (chapter three), the Harvard narrative (chapter five), techne (chapter six), rhetorical listening (chapter seven), place (chapter eleven), and community (chapter twelve) are just a few. Yet, the overarching argument of this collection is that how we present archival research to our students mirrors our own research ethics and the common goals of our field. The 'text-collaboration-activism' triad invites readers to (re)articulate and (re)evaluate the values that drive their research and teaching.

Works Cited

Lerner, Neal. "Archival Research as a Social Process." *Working in the Archives: Practical Research Methods for Rhetoric and Composition*, edited by Alexis E. Ramsey, Wendy B. Sharer, Barbara L'Eplattenier, and Lisa S. Mastrangelo, Southern Illinois UP, 2010, 195–205.

Translingual Inheritance: Language Diversity in Early National Philadelphia

Elizabeth Kimball
University of Pittsburgh Press, 2021, pp. 211

Reviewed by Lily Deen, Noha Labani, Lauren Piette, Vanessa Sullivan, and Heidi Willers
Arizona State University

Elizabeth Kimball's *Translingual Inheritance: Language Diversity in Early National Philadelphia* challenges the dominant account of the United States' founding, offering a counter-narrative that decenters the English language from the established historical tradition. Kimball argues that the United States has always been translingual, employing a wide range of integrated language practices and epistemologies. Using a translingual approach to explore "language as a network of cultural significations" (37), Kimball analyzes the ways in which speakers mobilize their multiple discursive repertoires to engage with networked and complex identities and communities. This translingual orientation reinterprets language as collective, less a singular uniform discourse/genre and more a conceptual space where language sources a multiplicity of discourses/genres that disrupt oppressive, socially constructed hierarchies and categories of languages. Kimball's groundbreaking use of translingual methods has earned recognition and honorary mention from both the Rhetoric Society of America Book Award for 2021 and the 2022 CCCC Outstanding Book Award Committee. Her work complements Jonathan Hall and colleague's *Translingual Identities and Transnational Realities in the U.S. College Classroom*, Steven Kellman's *Nimble Tongues: Studies in Literary Translingualism*, and Scott Wible's *Shaping Language Policy in the U.S.: The Role of Composition Studies*.

Building her argument on historical evidence of overlooked translingual practices, Kimball's project is a reimagining of U.S. history. Through her archival inquiry, Kimball is guided by the question: "what if?" What if we look at the whole history? Specifically, what if the nation had embraced translingualism? What if English was decentered in the modern-day nation? Taking a translingual approach to language and historical methodologies, Kimball examines the contributions to the foundation of U.S. democracy of three communities: Germans, Quakers, and free African Americans. These case studies point to the epistemic dynamics of language-based meaning-making. Across these case studies, Kimball highlights the fluidity of genre and the coexistence of diverse linguistic logics. She also challenges the assumptive monolingual status of both the historic and modern United States. Because Kimball foregrounds difference as an asset for a more just and equitable future, it is also an invaluable tool for approaching conflict wherever it arises. Hence, in this well-crafted volume, Kimball writes, not only for readers interested in language and literacy development of the fledgling nation, but also for scholars, students, and a broad public audience.

Chapters one and two introduce the book's methods and central concepts, highlighting Kimball's exploration of neglected archival records of early national Philadelphia, an integral time and space from which many founding documents emerged. Attuned to translingual social practices, Kimball's methods illuminate how people featured in her cases approached genres dynamically to coordinate activity within community networks of education, government, and religion. Her historical approach reveals the systemic biases that allowed English to assume its status as the only legitimate language of the United States. She rejects monolingual accounts of history and implicates the weaponization of language differences in both historical and contemporary contexts. Examination of these textual archives provides space for democratic invention to be viewed as dynamic, hopeful, and intentional, as the country's governance was not yet steeped in bureaucracy. Perhaps most importantly, Kimball's progressive methodology highlights what can be learned when we engage with history through a metalinguistic lens that attends to how we speak and think *about* language. Through the study of the language practices of multiple groups of people moving in time and space, the reader is given a window into the vast linguistic landscape that existed, thriving and interconnected, at the founding of this country.

To mediate this approach, Kimball uses her conceptions of commonplace, a cosmopolitan canopy, and spatiality as tools for translingual practice. Commonplaces provide readers with familiar anchors or locations one can use to approach an argument. Kimball interprets commonplace as means by which audiences "select or deselect how they will act in response to a message," make decisions, and arrange their thought processes (96). Indeed, commonplaces preserve a community's belief and cultural system as they flex to change and adapt. This important aspect of the book offers a conceptual space from which counternarratives may be read and written. The concept of a cosmopolitan canopy demonstrates space as a catalyst for belonging, facilitating communication even when people do not speak the same language. Early Philadelphia offers examples of these canopies. They are not only diverse, but also familiar in that ". . . people feel equal ownership" of them (124). Citing Philadelphia's historic Reading Market and building from the work of sociologist Elijah Anderson, Kimball notes the canopy "offers the promise of edification for all who enter. Within a cosmopolitan canopy, exposure to others' humanity generates empathy; fears dissipate, and [the grounds] for mutual appreciation appear" (Anderson qtd. in Kimball 125). This concept informs Kimball's attention to sameness and difference as they produce spatiality throughout the book. In service of Kimball's translingual approach, spatiality demonstrates how the act of communication transcends "formal, recognizable, and inevitable language boundaries" (6). Spatiality draws attention to four realms: the divine (the realness of the divine in material space); the bodily (the construction of meaning that takes place between an audience and a speaker); the geographic (the physical proximity of races and how this proximity might betray systems of segregation); and the hermeneutic (the latter referring to the positions of rhetoricians "in relation to their interpretations of texts . . .") (142–143). Temporal spatiality refers to how translingual practices are situated, networked, mediated, and integrated intertextually among resources, environments, and individuals over time. Temporal spatiality further opens the opportunity to understand how linguistic performance and meaning is constructed beyond traditional conceptions.

In chapter three, "Language and Education Among Philadelphia Germans," Kimball investigates how this community used and theorized the educational value of the German language in the fifteenth through eighteenth centuries. German was levied as a means for accessing religion, art, and intellectualism; moreover, multilingualism offered access to multiple meanings and even more complicated worldviews. Insisting that exact translation is often impossible when approaching biblical or spiritual texts, Kimball explores the correlation between cultural losses and language loss. Kimball examines historical archives, such as the *Evangelisches Magazin*, that highlight the need to preserve German in light of the limited ideological capacities of English (favored for utilitarian and economic practices and deliberations). In the context of this case, the ideological access that the German language offered to early Philadelphians provided an exemplary system for alternative ideological perspectives, as German made the conception of a wide array of cultural and religious knowledges accessible to the general public. Kimball highlights a time period when translingualism was an everyday part of the Philadelphia community, as well as a topic of debate in early school development. This context presents the potential for an alternative translingual present where English is decentered, and functions as one of many possibilities that may fuel the development of more diverse educational projects, governmental policies, and communities.

In chapter four, "Quakerly Genres and The Language of Liberal Learning," Kimball scrutinizes the Quakers' *Ascham Essays*, a collection of tracts from the 1830s proposing changes to the curriculum at Haverford College. In a period when the Quakers were re-assessing their sense of identity in the wake of the factional split between the Hicksite and Orthodox Quakers, the *Ascham Essays* manifested a common point of access for local Quakers to re-interpret their conservative resistance to classical education and classical language studies. By reinterpreting commonplace texts and synthesizing these insights with concepts from the Scottish Enlightenment, the *Ascham Essays* generated a conceptual space for community members to advocate for the teaching of classical languages, especially Latin. This translingual framework highlights how the Quakers came to promote language diversity. To elucidate those assumptions, Kimball compares the *Ascham Essays* to the *Yale Report* from the same time period. Both documents advocated for teaching classical languages, especially Latin; however, the Quakers' logic differed vastly from Yale's. In response to the calls for modernizing the curriculum, the *Yale Report* tied (the study of) classical languages to the formation of "correct taste and nationalism" or the creation of an ideal citizen. In contrast, the *Ascham Essays* approached language as a means of knowing, that is, as mode and method for inquiring into truth and for ending disputes. Though the genre conventions of Ascham's work and the *Yale Report* are quite similar, Kimball elucidates vital differences in the aims of the two documents.

Kimball opens chapter five, "African American Language," with a discussion of African American educational and literacy networks that existed and created space for the voices, writings, and genres of African American Philadelphians during the nineteenth and twentieth centuries. Beyond formal school settings, the African American community created several informal social networks with the goal of developing intellectual, spiritual, and scientific connections among its members. Against this backdrop, Kimball explores the writings of former slave and preacher Richard Allen who founded the African Methodist Episcopal Church in 1816. Through the examination of his text *The Life, Experience, and Gospel Labours of the Rt. Rev. Richard Allen*, this chapter tackles the ways in which genre form can provide spaces for re-situating power in fluid and unexpected ways. Through his inventive and intertextual writing, Allen shifted social and spatial imaginings. Kimball argues that Allen's work gave him access to different domains of knowing and seeing the world, and in turn, granted him greater control over his audience's reading of legal, spiritual, and political states (156). Allen's acumen in genre fluidity enabled him to reimagine and reconstitute divine, bodily, geographic, and hermeneutic spaces. Kimball engages the concept of the cosmopolitan canopy to illustrate Allen's translingual approach to communication—an approach that was shared, collectively built, and open to interactions of sameness and difference. In this way, Kimball's examination of Allen's legacy offers a hopeful what-if "model of what social relationships could become" (157).

Kimball's central argument, to rethink history through a translingual framework, provides readers with a lens that opens up new possibilities for expansive world-building and a more diverse future. Through the use of accessible language, Kimball takes the readers by the hand to thoroughly explain her approach, not assuming a baseline or comprehensive knowledge of her subject matter. The book's approachability is consistently seen through the easily discernible points of clarification provided to readers. Through the use of reader-friendly concepts and case studies, Kimball's book prompts audiences to consider the relevance of the presented ideas to their own inquiries, interests, and experiences. As reviewers, we believe that this book will benefit researchers, scholars, teachers, and graduate students alike, as the book can be used as a tool to approach and tackle modern day challenges through mediating linguistic difference. Readers interested in direct application of Kimball's approach will find the conclusion instructive. There she takes up pedagogies that elicit students' situated knowledge as resources for problem solving. What is most translingual about Kimball's own mode of being is her capacity to shuttle across the social categories that her method both invokes and rewrites.

With *Translingual Inheritance*, Kimball has brought to the forefront significant forms of language diversity and language epistemologies that have been ignored within the mainstream historical tradition. Although Kimball situated her book in the disciplines of linguistics and history, her translingual approach extends beyond these disciplines. This text helped the reviewers consider the principles of belonging in Dr. Elenore Long's graduate global rhetorics course at Arizona State University. We find Kimball's work invaluable to our current cultural and historical moment, as it can inform new approaches to inclusive and diverse social justice practices. In a time of divisive rhetoric, *Translingual Inheritance* offers a framework to unite the U.S. across differences. A solution to address the nation's division is to examine its translingual heritage and to learn from previously overlooked narratives. Additionally, Kimball's sense of the cosmopolitan canopy offers an imaginative path forward for a divided nation. Rather than adhering to a narrative that insists on a monolinguistic point of view, which weaponizes the English language by diminishing the rich translingual roots of the United States, we can embrace language diversity as an asset to ignite other ways of thinking, problem solving, and being. Kimball shows that a more holistic reading of the past has the potential to provide an antidote for our present challenges.

Talking Back: Senior Scholars and Their Colleagues Deliberate the Past, Present, and Future of Writing Studies

*Edited by Norbert Elliot
and Alice S. Horning*
Utah State University Press, 2020, pp. 442

Reviewed by Heidi M. Williams
Tennessee State University

Imagine the reunion tour, getting the band back together to create new music, while playing some of the old favorites. Perhaps the rumors are true: the band suggests this is their final performance—the very last time anyone will see them on stage. *Talking Back: Senior Scholars and Their Colleagues Deliberate the Past, Present, and Future of Writing Studies* is a collection of essays, edited by Norbert Elliot and Alice S. Horning, that feels like that much-anticipated last show. The senior scholars who have contributed so significantly to the field of writing studies harmonize with early and mid-career scholars to present the familiar tones we are used to, along with the voices of rising artists who will continue their legacies. The overarching purpose of the book is "to document a reflective vision of senior colleagues, approaching or passing the age of retirement, on the ways their unique programs of research have influenced our discipline and to spark the imagination of their successors in charting future directions for writing studies in which difference, not homogeneity, is the aim" (6). The editors and contributors achieve their purpose in this collection.

Situated in life-span writing, aging, and seniority, the text is a thorough compilation of discussions within writing studies by some of the most respected scholars in the field. The authors ask the following: "'What are the influences—intellectual, social, emotional, physical, even spiritual—that affect a scholar's development over time,' in addition to 'how do we address the tension between continuity and change in a scholar's life, in a discipline, in schools and universities, and in society?'" (140). And yet, what makes this text more than one lengthy, ultimately unanswerable rhetorical question—and unlike any other text we might find in our field—is the conversational, autobiographical genre employed by the contributors. The chapters are organized with two to three authors per chapter, with the senior scholar speaking first and the new or mid-career scholar responding back.

Compiling chapters with past and present voices functions to facilitate conversations among like-minded scholars, teachers, and administrators. As such, I can imagine musicians working in similar genres sitting on a festival stage, ruminating about the past, pontificating about the present, and musing about the future. Ruth Ray Karpen, riffing on Mary Catherine Bateson, professes that one of the most significant aspects of the collection is that not only are two or more "generations of writing scholars looking forward and backward together, but the senior scholars are demonstrating a variety of ways to spend one's 'second maturity' in academe" (5). Yet, much like a music festival with fifty-one line-ups, this text is organized such that readers can camp out, attend the shows in order, or leave and return at a later time. So, while the text is carefully and thoughtfully organized, as a reader, I felt like I could, in fact, read in chunks, pulling out one of the relevant twenty-two chapters, and revisiting sections that most grabbed my attention and spurred my curiosity. As a method of intentional design, the editors requested William Marcellino, a professor of text-based analytics and behavioral science, review the book's linguistic, cultural, and substantive patterns to pinpoint recurring themes, activities, and structures by which to organize it (10). Thus, within the book, as within our broader field, there are four Classification of Instructional Programs (CIP) categories represented: 1) General Writing; 2) Creative Writing; 3) Professional, Technical, Business, and Scientific Writing; 4) Rhetoric and Composition (7). Furthermore, readers can expect eight curated themes throughout the text: capability, deliberation, generativity, identity, language, legacy, origin, and seniority. As a reader, I would add the themes of civility, community, empowerment, and growth to the list.

The editors and authors imagined their audience to be three-fold: writing studies students, scholars and teachers, and individuals across disciplines who are drawn to seniority studies. Due to the range of topics discussed, I feel certain this text would be an invaluable resource in a doctoral-level rhetoric and composition course. I began my doctoral program in rhetoric and composition in 2007, when many of the senior scholars in this edited collection were in their prime. That being said, the most senior contributors in the text worked in the profession even a decade before I was born (for example, John C. Brereton who "looks back over a fifty-year career teaching writing" and William Condon who "began administering writing programs in the late 1970s") (141). All of these seasoned scholars reflect on the historical developments that have shaped the field, the present state of writing studies, and the future challenges and opportunities facing the discipline.

Martha A. Townsend's chapter, "Valuing New Approaches for Tenure and Promotion for WAC/WID Scholar/Administrators" resonated the most with me. Townsend is currently a professor emerita, so her contribution to the book is an absolute gift to readers because she is writing outside of the demands of any publishing requirement. While most of the chapters are grounded in reflection, Townsend boldly calls our profession to action, suggesting that "It is time for departments, programs, and institutions to examine this literature, rethink policies, and evaluate WAC/WID WPAs in ways appropriate for their scholarly/administrative work" (326). Townsend is bold in her chapter, and I suspect that the tone of resilience, justice, and urgency derives from her thirty-year career and the liberty she now has absent of the publish or perish mentality under which she labored.

Despite her prolific presence in writing studies, Townsend outlines her struggles and unseen labor as a WPA—especially with regard to tenure and promotion policies and practices. She reveals the harsh reality of her tenure and promotion processes in which her "department did not support either bid" for associate or full professor (328). Townsend's bid for full professor "spanned sixteen months, including fifteen separate votes (eleven of which were negative) and seven appeal hearings. The final three levels of evaluation (campus, provost, and chancellor) initially garnered negative votes but were overturned on appeal—and those are the votes that secured" her promotion to the full professor (328). Here we are, ten years later after her 2013 appeal, still making the same arguments in the field. In fact, although my PhD in rhetoric and composition was heavily grounded in WPA coursework and training, I have chosen to take a back seat in terms of this work at my institution because of the workload expectations, service requirements, and the institution's drive to transition to an R1 institution. I fear that the work for WPAs and WAC administrators has a long road ahead, but Townsend's chapter provides clear and tangible advice to those who are seeking tenure and promotion (330).

My greatest takeaway in the book comes from Judy Buchanan and Richard Sterling's chapter, "Learning from the National Writing Project as a Kindergarten-University Partnership." Buchanan and Sterling reflect on the professional development and community-engaged lessons they learned from the National Writing Project through the principle that "teachers of writing must write" (77). This dictum is at the core of my professional identity and reminds me of why I entered this field: my love of writing and desire to teach other people how to love writing. I also found Doug Hesse's (who, ironically, chaired my dissertation director's dissertation, as we are here to reflect on lineage) visual timeline of dissertations of WPA executive board members from 1976–2002 incredibly valuable. The timeline is the first graphic I have encountered that offers a lateral unfolding of the trajectory of writing studies.

Overall, this edited collection speaks softly to those who have done their time, and boldly to those entering the field. I sensed a melancholy tone from some of the senior scholars, as they are maturing into their next phase of life—be it in a classroom or in retirement. And yet, as someone who is only ten years into my tenure-track position, I found myself gripped by the responses—as though my peers are calling me to action. Hugh Burns exhorts his successors to recognize that "our scholarship is far from done" (91). In "Framing and Facing Histories of Rhetoric and Composition" Cinthia Gannett calls us to "see that our living archives, their collected papers, and their micro-histories hold the messiness and specificity of the last fifty years; they need to be preserved, honored, and accessed, or they will be lost to future generations who want to understand this period in human terms" (148). There will never be another collection in our field like this, nor could there be. I feel so thankful for this curation of voices before the voices become echoes.

Works Cited

Bateson, Mary Catherine. *Composing a Further Life: The Age of Active Wisdom*. Vintage Books, 2010.

Coda

Coda Editorial Collective Introduction

Kefaya Diab, Chad Seader, Alison Turner, and Stephanie Wade

The six texts that follow teach us how community writing can shape spaces and places. While Coda originated as a way to preserve the creative work that ensues from community writing projects, these texts do so much more. They embody and resist the material effects of institutional spaces that are often shaped by racist, white-supremacist ideologies; structured by ultra-competitive, punitive systems; and scarred by extractivist models of production. These pieces demonstrate community writing as a tool for survival by making legible the fuzzy boundaries between ideological spaces and physical places and by insisting that readers look. We are grateful to these authors for sharing their work with us and grateful to you for reading.

We open with Stephen Paur's multimedia piece, "Tucson House: Visual Echoes," a composite photograph of a large apartment building in southern Arizona that offers shelter to people many of us are trained to look away from. Just as Paur's image is one piece of a greater project—the image is composed out of a still from a video that uses voice-over storytelling—the "visual echoes" he creates of Tucson House makes visible multiple spaces and places within a single structure, an echo that, in Paur's words, invites us "to try not to blink." Adam Craig's poem, "Storms," similarly weaves together confinement and openness in prison and home while he feeds the birds. Though the narrator is physically stuck in one place, his practice creates a meaningful space that allows him to connect with the memories of relationships and the world around him in the present, past, and future.

Alexandra Melnick's short story, "The Man Who Lived on Rose Street," depicts a place inflected by a different passing of time as some people leave and others stay. While the reasons for this vary—urban planning, natural disasters, economic change, and gentrification—the story conveys both the difficulty and the value of maintaining community in the midst of and in spite of these larger changes.

In response to racist realities and during the isolation era of COVID-19, Ada Vilageliu Díaz's piece, "Becoming," illustrates the continued importance of creative decolonial spaces. She, her students, and the families with whom they work use books and writing workshops to create a space of resistance to racism. Discussing books by Black, Indigenous, and People of Color (BIPOC) and creating their own books allows them to perform identity and culture and to build space for others to do so. Performance as creative resistance emerges in Nic Nusbaumer's essay, "I Won American Idol," as well. Performing in a place seemingly dominated by consumer culture, Nusbaumer wins on his own terms, in the language of his choice, conveying the power of love and enlarging the cultural space of a midwestern suburb to make room for his identity as Filipino and as American.

Colorado State University's Community Literacy Center (CLC) composed a poem written collaboratively by students trained as community writing facilitators, using a process that centers their workshop spaces. Inspired by the methods of Ocean Voung, the poems in the collection reflect many of the obstacles and challenges facing new writers in community writing, like rising above silence and feeling comfortable around strangers. By composing these poems in community, the CLC interns establish inclusive practices that deconstruct social barriers.

As we reflect on the work in this edition of Coda, we consider the affordances–and limitations–of community writing in allowing people to reshape spaces in ways that might beget a greater degree of freedom. As you read these pieces, we urge you to linger in these texts and in the spaces and places you inhabit, to write, and to let us know what happens.

Tucson House: Visual Echoes

Stephen Paur

Reflection

"Afterimage," noun: "The enduring impression of a vivid sensation after the initial stimulus has ceased." Like glimpsing the sun, then scrunching your eyes defensively only to find it re-inscribed on your retinas. Like watching a movie and, after the final scene cuts to black, still being haunted by the power of that last frame, still feeling it in your stomach, on your nerve endings.

Likewise, this image — a digital composite — is an afterimage, of sorts. I composed it after-the-fact using still frames from a short documentary video about Tucson House, a 17-story public housing building in southern Arizona for the elderly, disabled, and formerly unhoused. The title of the video, like the still frames themselves, lingers: "Status Update: COVID-19 & the Politics of Disposability."

Produced during the early months of the pandemic, in 2020, the video (bit. ly/3LPLz07) features voiceovers by three residents who report on their experiences. They describe their own afterimages, evoking what they've heard, felt, and been witness to so far. The fear, confusion, tedium, vulnerability. The stubborn optimism.

At the center of it all—figuratively, but also, in this composite image, literally—is a stealthy, sinister pathogen. Microscopic, normally unseen, it's made visible here. But that visibility, like anything, has a shelf life. It's there until you look away.

Or will we still see it? Still carry it with us? Still carry *them* with us, those too often made to carry unshoulderable burdens on their own?

Afterimages refuse the prevailing logics of disposability that allow us—encourage us, even—to treat empathy and awareness like single-use plastics. Often, we indulge in them as long as it makes us feel good, then throw them away, forgetting our abiding interdependence, ignoring the fact that, as MLK, Jr. memorably put it, "Injustice anywhere is a threat to justice everywhere. We are caught in an inescapable network of mutuality, tied in a single garment of destiny. Whatever affects one directly, affects all indirectly." Afterimages invite us to directly confront the indirectness of our embeddedness. They ask us to find common cause with those whose pain and struggles are no less real for being distant or hidden. They ask us to reflect on just where, exactly, this "away" is to which we throw things and consign people.

My apartment is two blocks from Tucson House, a towering structure that looms over the neighborhood. It's impossible to ignore it. Still, I often find myself looking in another direction. Even someone like me, with the building staring down at him matter-of-factly, morning to night, can't win the staring contest. I always get distracted. I always blink.

This composite image was part of a conscious effort to try—for a few more moments, at least—to hold it, the building and what it represents, in my hand. To familiarize myself more memorably with its distinctive, angular contours, their repetitions, their inversions. To ask just what it (and the people inside) seemed to be asking of me. To try not to blink.

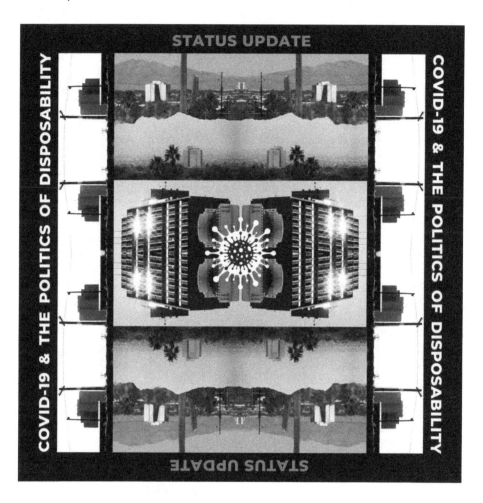

Author Bio

Stephen Paur is a writing teacher and Ph.D. candidate in Rhetoric, Composition, and the Teaching of English at the University of Arizona. His research areas are the rhetoric of climate change, the politics of language and literacy, and the history of writing technologies.

Storms

Adam Craig

Reflection

During a flash nonfiction class, we were given a prompt to write about something on the compound, preferably something outside or natural. I thought of the ibises that showed up one day to join the pigeons and turkey vultures. My original draft focused on my interactions with the ibises, but when a friend read the piece he thought the birds were a euphemism for my biological family. That became the nucleus for creating the woven fabric between my two families, and the thoughts, feelings and emotions they evoke.

I wonder if they miss me. If they realize I left Food Service six months ago. If anyone cares for them the way I did.

Every morning after breakfast I dug through discarded cabbage cores, inedible outer leaves and pinto bean juice to unearth the treasures. I flung heels of spongy white bread like skipping rocks across a glassy lake, and they waited. Long, down-curved bills speared bread slices. They'd strut away on spindly stems, non-pescatarian catches in tow.

Rarely confused for the regal heron or beautiful egret, the ibis is the physical outcast of the wading bird family tree. Toughness and character are not bound by beauty, nor is the ibis. The last wildlife to take shelter before a hurricane arrives; the first to reappear when the winds subside.

Pigeons, magpies and tiny finches parked on the periphery of the bread buffet, in deference to ibises. Bagels mauled by daggered beaks. Cranberry scones shredded to crumbs.

Solar rays cut through the morning haze of the eastern sky, erasing remnants of last night's rain. Ibises gathered and multiplied, from two to six and six to twelve, cautiously approaching, appetites swallowing care and concern.

I wonder why they're so far inland. If they felt about me like I felt about them. If our time together was a memory.

These moments slide into thoughts of family that collide in places unseen and sounds unheard, only to escape without a trace.

I wonder if they miss me. If they realize I've been gone for nine years. If they think of me as I think of them.

I sift reds and greens and yellow hues of produce, displaying marbled proteins and earthen grains. Slicing and dicing, sautéing aromas of ginger, baby bok choy and oyster mushrooms wok-sizzled in peanut oil. Stir-fried love served on plates, in bowls. Memories of nightly family dinners and conversations stretching beyond the midnight hour. I can't recall what we talked about, but I remember feeling that I mattered, that I was safe, that I belonged. And now...I'm lost and alone...drifting.

Family support ebbs like the evening tide lapping the shore, continually eroding my fractured relationships. Remnants of hope are the tides of tomorrow.

I wonder if they'll be here when the storm ends. If I can find my way back. If all that remains are euthanized memories.

Author Bio

Adam Craig has been communicating through the written word since sending postcards home to his parents as a young boy from summer camp, but he is relatively new to the world of publishing. His preferred genre is flash nonfiction, where he can mine adventures from a beautifully chaotic life to tell his story. He looks forward to returning to the physically-free world in 2030 after sharing 17 years with the Florida Department of Corrections. Any literary success can be attributed to the influence and impact Exchange for Change has made on his life.

The Man Who Lived on Rose Street

Alexandra Melnick

Reflection

Around the time I moved back to Jackson, Mississippi, a group of volunteers came together to create and maintain some hiking trails in a previously abandoned area of the neighborhood I lived in. As the woods in our neighborhood became increasingly excavated and more abandoned structures and artifacts were uncovered, this story took shape. Renting and ultimately owning a home in this area, called Belhaven, was the fulfillment of a long and tightly held dream of mine. My partner and I, in addition to a few longtime friends, like to spend time cleaning and walking these trails. I am proud of this community effort and am also aware that this development is part of a larger conversation about equity, belonging, and what it means to share space with everyone in our city since Belhaven is a neighborhood with a complicated relationship to race and class.

It was strange to build a community alongside of dismantling the remains of another, and the experience was made stranger still by the fact that this was all taking place right by our own homes. Today, the hiking trails are a cherished part of our community, and I am still looking for the stories underneath. This story is part of that, and a partial love letter and apology to people who move in and out of that place.

There was a man who lived on Rose Street.

This seems, and is, a fairly normal sentence. In a sense, every man on every Rose Street lives what is a statistically normal life. We all do. (Most of us.) We're made up of the tiny parcels of the ordinary, blended together to create extraordinary, unique experiences, prisms catching the perfectly, blessedly, magnificently ordinary light. (It's a miracle it happens at all and all the time.)

This man we're describing is absolutely ordinary for a man living in our century. So let's differentiate him.

There is a man who lived on Rose Street. A man who sat by his apartment window and waved every morning to a woman who drove home from the gym or an early errand. It was something you could set a clock by. This waving was his function in the morning, almost a duty, and it helped him keep his world up. It became a ritual, a comforting slice of time between two people who only knew each other by their blurry periphery shapes going by.

This man was known to pedestrians and cars alike as the man who sat in a red patio chair, known to his landlord as the tenant who occupied apartment B (rent 850, thank you very much), and known to the many fluctuating denizens of his apartment complex as a quiet neighbor. To the man himself, in his mind's eye, he wasn't just an older sloughing shape, or a man moving in a one bedroom apartment, or the absence his days held. Sometimes, he was a quick, darting thing. Something close to still a boy if he held his shape in his mind.

That boy lived on Rose Street. Which is actually no longer there now. It's not on any current map, printed or digital. In an orderly, organized sense of the word or world, this street is not a place you can even now locate with a zip code or by noticing a mailbox. It's not a delineated space that has somewhere in it a fridge or a dining room table, or anything that belongs to the immediate present tense of household meals and the irrepressible tangle of human bodies and that which comes with it. Rose Street is now an old cul-de-sac resting in the woods wayside. The pavement is worn through, and up over ahead on the highway, the cars rush by.

They turned it into an overpass exit. Which is actually a fairly normal sentence, despite the fact that it's anything but if you experience that process.

Standing on the worn gravel road amidst the trees now, you'd mainly notice the noise and some things with metal and rusting materials sticking out. Sometimes, it's a homeless encampment. It was also the place the boy turned man lived, a street that used to be by the woods and now is not wholly the woods, but something halfway of it, something restless, waiting, and forgotten even by the people who made encampments nearby. Once, by the nearest foundation structures to the river (which is now like the back of a buried victim: tilted, resting, waiting to be discovered) there used to be a house. A yard. There used to be a family, who once in 1963 gave their nine-year-old son the best metal detector their budget could buy.

———

"What is it," shrieked Leo to a tow-headed girl. Frantic with joy and an almost anxiety, the pair's fingernails bit into, worried, pleaded the clay and sand at the edge of his yard. Then, they paused.

"It's a rock?"

She kept digging, while occasionally putting her dirty fingers near her mouth, smudging soil onto her lips. Leo was lost in wonder and in the possibility of lost treasure, his daydreams interspersed by mechanical tinny beeping. Were they explorers of a lost civilization, having come from the future to gaze upon what works they may? It struck him that perhaps all lost treasure stories were similar to alien invader stories, an ancient lost land suddenly interrupted by people and marvels beyond their dreams. Everybody knows somebody who can clearly see their world's end. Maybe it was the same. In school, he was learning about how America was formed as America, and as his friend's fingers continued to shovel, stumbling on rocks, worms, and other secret creatures, Leo thought for the first time that the house on Rose Street, maybe even Rose Street itself, wasn't entirely his.

"I think it's a marble. . . ."
Dirt piled up around their shoes, creating miniature mountain ranges.
"No! A toy car!"

A sudden sigh shot out of both of them. It was *his* toy car, lost three summers ago. A small, smushed tin thing bought downtown, in a store that was no longer even located in Jackson. Ancient history.

They left it there.

———

The man on Rose Street walked around the lot behind his apartment. In the wilted rough green, you could see him pace, pause, glance, the breeze just passing over his shoulders. This communal quasi-yard was by some definitions pitiful, a few pits and patches of grass in a parking lot with cement, beer cans, and shards of corrugated tin poking out like the nose of a loyal dog waiting by the door, growing closer and closer every year to his home. The cans waited for the yard to become familiar to them, wholly them. Children ran wildly through the parking lot and surrounding neglected spots, into abandoned lots repurposed as public spaces by the city. The lot wasn't really a yard. To the man, this was a paradise, a few stolen patches of Belhaven, land that seemed as vast as the face of the wristwatch his father had. A paradise in miniature, just like the silent, ticking world of the clock. Powerful.

The neighborhood used to seem orderly, as if each home lined up like numbers on a watch and children rotated through like hands. He thought sometimes it was like he fell through a glass one day and this new world of Belhaven, Alice in Wonderland-esque, broke his fall. Strange. New. Broken water pipes and fire hydrants replaced the adults he knew as a child, the ones who walked around the neighborhoods and seemed so tall. Things here were so low to the ground now, so much of the streets showing a worn baldheaded sky, pockets rubbed through.

All things considered though, this world was alright with him. The man often turned over in his head a dreamlike image of those from his past still living inside a cosmic wristwatch, dialed and moving clockwise, oblivious to the disappearance of a boy who usually was outside. In his best moments, he imagined he lived on the strap then, attached to the heart of the ticking world and holding it together, making it make sense and giving the gears shifting some meaning, some significance and purpose to the world. That was fine. That was his lot.

"Mine," the man echoed.

———

"To write, to do," thought Leo as he sat in his Bailey Middle School classroom. They were conjugating and subjugating verbs. Outside the window were junky cars; new cars; and brownish, goldish, greenish vans running by. It seemed to Leo a better task to count and catalog these cars then listing out the building blocks of the English language. To look too closely at words, thought the boy, was to perhaps uncover some wires, some essential patio mesh screen that kept the world straight up. Too much poking and wearing would result in fingers cutting through. He imagined golden bars entitled "verbs," "nouns," and "participles" hidden in the basement crawlspace of some scholar somewhere, holding treasures to be brought out and shown only a few times a year and otherwise kept safe. Like most discovered things, they might be messed up or taken away by nefarious or well intended do-gooders or at the very least perhaps lose their specialness. No, things like what makes the meaning out of the noises of our mouths and tongues were better left alone, decided Leo.

Or, that's what he faintly recalled thinking years later.

You see, Leo did not like being reminded he was a "to," an infinitive verb that was alive and could be coupled with something next or to be put in place of, something left hanging and waiting for a next sentence and direction in which to run.

The word "coupled" suddenly loomed large in his mind, like pink candy or the hood of a new car, an aching sweetness. Solid until you knock, and then your knees feel like they might give way. His cheeks prickled, but he couldn't stop the runaway-thought train of his sentences before it was too late.

The girl he grew up with was just a few infinitive sentences away from him. To get up, to walk, to go into the third row, and to whisper into her ear—

"Leo," tentatively called his teacher, a youngish woman. Nervous, blurry in a vague way, like the shape of a flock of birds, something impossibly small and yet large in his view and mind's eye. She was new, and yet seemed like she'd been a Bailey Middle School teacher for all of time.

"L-Leo?"

"Yes, m'am."

". . . Pay attention."

———

Leo was walking the Belhaven woods. Fifty years later, the man who lived on Rose Street would walk the same land, which was now an outskirt of city parks and walking trails. Leo and the man both intimately knew (and these two selves were linked by this knowledge) that the real treasure and heart of this neighborhood lay not in the houses, the shops, the Eudora's, but inside the tangle and expanse of river and forest giving way to the water, a birth and a backwards.

Jackson is a river city.

Just like when he was Leo, the man could feel the dirt, smelling like wet and rust. He rejoiced in the sudden cool wafts of air coming through, and in the way the world changes when you reach the part through the trees. Even standing in front of the cultivated gap in the trail's walkway, you could sense something feral. It's the night kissing the perimeters of day all out of order. The inside and opposite of coming home.

When the boy was Leo, he was a dreamer.

Then he was a grown man.

The man who sometimes slipped and called himself privately the Man who *lives* on Rose Street. Not lived, and instead something short of an infinitive verb.

———

His "driving woman," as he called her, was rounding the corner.
Her actual name, which the man would later come to think didn't suit her but would never admit it, was Carmella.

Carmella pushed her choppy bangs out of her eyes and pulled into the intersection between Monroe and her street, frustrated at the way her broken rearview mirror just ever so slightly obscured her field of vision and thus rendered the car window completely useless. She loved walking her street and hated how fast it went when she had to drive it, unable to note the certain depressions in the road, the hidden mud nestled like a closed hand waiting to give up secrets. The Yazoo clay.

However, she didn't want her car's tire to become a permanent fixture of it.

Her eyes darted up to the apartment complex as she passed, a reflex.

This time, he waved first.

Carmella wanted to let out a whoop of joy but couldn't, unable to explain to herself how this small interaction brought a balance to the start of her day. It was like taming an animal, making a map of new or lost places, and having a secret, all rolled into one and happening at once. She didn't even know what the older man looked like other than brief impressions, didn't think about him much beyond this daily interaction, but she did know she desperately wanted to plant roots in this neighborhood. This seemed like a start.

Two hands, mirroring each other for a single moment, an ellipses and oracle, in the place where so many streets and faces have come and gone, something close to the creation of solid ground.

———

Many days, the man just waited. He had retired from his maintenance job with the city, after slowly rising through the ranks to work in the office, then became a middling manager. He had graduated from high school, and even then his innate intelligence was often overshadowed by a desire to go outside, to see the ways the woods worked. When the man thought of his brief educational career, he saw a tall, red-haired boy walking home from Murrah High School on what now seems like blurry, rolling, waving roads.

During the course of his life, he got a girl pregnant. He incidentally got another one pregnant but she left the state and it didn't stick. His days were at the library, the art museum, stretches of staying home. Around him, Belhaven Heights was growing, sprawling, turning in on itself with the sinkholes covering the roads like water-stains and nicks on a worn table. It became something unlike the entity (almost a self) he had always fixed solidly in his mind.

Much like people often do, he watched Rose Street lose its neighbors to jobs, white flight, and other impacts of integration. (Or was it forced desegregation?) He watched the houses get moved into by students, and then folks not exactly down on their luck but teetering on it, and then as the city smoldered in the furnace of the state, folks without any luck (and usually because of someone's design) moved in, and then when they were gone the trees were all.

He wondered how many children in the city knew about the woods here. How many flew through on their bikes, laughing as the rough roads inside the forest sometimes made them bounce or fall, how many children picked themselves up again inside of here. How many walked along the water and gazed at the imprints it made on the land? How many children today can say they know Jackson is a river city?

When Carmella moved here, she didn't know anything.

———

What is a street if a city doesn't exist? What's the bones of the house when the street is gone? It reminded Leo of a man who ambled on High Street, resplendent with a gold tooth shining in his otherwise empty mouth.

———

His parents were arguing again.

Late at night (or so it seemed to Leo), the lamps took on a sinister, yellow hue, a high pitched whine sort of color, and he saw it like sealant encasing his cracked open door.

"moving,"
"people gone,"
"what choice"
"dangerous,"
"highway,"
"what type of life will they have—"

"stay."

It all came rumbling through Leo's head. In his bed, the words marched inside his head and made a home with him inside the room, helping him set up a camp on his floor. Leo lay still in his flannel sheets and marked the days as the words slowly began to dominate the conversations in the daytime, becoming part of everyone's house too.

During that time, he sometimes woke up and found himself on the floor. Closer to the action, to the tiny base camp that controlled his neighbor's lives. The ground. When Leo thought back to those interludes, he saw that as a child he compartmentalized them, kept them separate and out of time to what he perceived as his normal life. He still wasn't sure why, even as an older man far away from the march of the moving words.

This he did know, even if it took him much of his life to figure it out—those arguments were the first signs that Rose Street was packing up. It folded up in handfuls, like flowers wilting on the dining room table. It boarded up like a hurt face. It began to wander. The street was scarring and healing into a new body, feet deep in strange river beds.

In the end, they had their way. Both the words, the families, and the forces swirling around their lives. The overpass was built. The people scattered into new subdivisions, built new streets, created new lives on the newly shaky foundation that they had survived what they were trying to fight for.

Leo always wondered what had happened to his house.

———

When Carmella moved to Leo's street in Belhaven Heights, she found abandoned houses, a wealth of older neighbors, and the omnipresent smell of smoke drifting in from fast food chains nearby. She also found him, out of the corner of her eye and only in slight recollections. A man who always waved to her, a fixture just like a tree at the end of the street.

As the days went by and Carmella settled into her house, Leo slowly disappeared. He stopped registering in her consciousness, and became blips and blots upon her sight line. For his part, he didn't mind.

It worked for him. It's what the neighbors on this transient street had always done, the people in truth not quite neighbors but instead an assemblage of souls who happened to make their way through.

But then came the flood.

——————

The ravenous thing.

As it rained, sudden spurts of water erupted all over Belhaven Heights and hopelessly complicated the tangle of cars, trash cans, living creatures, and garbage that live in and around the streets. When the season's sudden flood rushed in, Carmella was rounding the corner of her street. Just before the sky opened up, she saw Leo in her rearview mirror, sitting in his red camping chair on the apartment complex balcony. The last thought she had before the water came was a wondering, briefly, stirring in her mind at the secret lives we all must lead. How she was late, who was in the ambulance she had passed by earlier, who lived in other houses hidden by weeds and trash on the street and why. The next thing she thought was an embodied sensation, an animal aliveness as the rain shook her car.

She never thought storms could be so hard, so rough, so much like a fist. A hidden hand, a sucker punch to her already cracked windshield.

A few blurry moments.

A reflex, her foot off of the brake. Watery noises sprung up around. Dimly, she recalled flipping in the pool over and over again as a child, chlorine shooting up her nose. The water outside wasn't high. She could easily walk home. But her car—

Leo, the man who lived on Rose Street, put out a cigarette. As he rose, he saw a car puffing and chugging along through the water, a yellow light in the crack of rain curtains.

She was there. Her head rested against the wheel, a moment of frustration, a prayer. The water was pushing against her car now, trash cans floating close, and other debris advanced menacingly. For the first time, he saw her not in movement, in driving, in passing by.

"She's really quite young," Leo wondered. A smile.

Leaning against the iron wrought railing, rain coated his bare legs. Splatters, mirroring the eddies whirling below. He may not live on Rose Street anymore, he mused.

He felt the gap in his chest, an old home, an admitting.

But he lived here.

His street needed help. A neighbor needed help. He could be part of it, part of the fabric of this new strange street made of days gone by, little moments in a bigger life, new-old houses and Jackson stories told in foreign tongues.

There are simple things and there are hard things in this life.

For Leo, it was the simple thing to help her, take her door and help shield her from the knee-high water. The hard thing was what comes next.

The simple thing was to walk down, even if he was unsure. The simple thing was to wade through the water, to approach the red car on the driver's side, shield his face from the rain with one hand and hold the other one open to her.

It was a marvel that what came next wasn't the hardest part of all. It came out like faucet water.

"Do you need help, don't worry, I live down the street here—"

"I know," Carmella said clearly.

"You know?"

"Yes."

"Okay, well, um—"

"You're my friend. You're the one I always wave to, the man at the entrance of Lorraine Street."

"Well, let's get you home."

She held out her hand.

When they joined hands, when old Leo heaved, ushered her to the car park after hitting the hazards on her dashboard, he didn't notice she was crying.

They stood under the narrow overhang of his parking lot, holding and hiding out. He held out a cigarette.

She nodded.

"It's nice to have a neighbor, a friendly person who lives on our street."

Leo had to admit.

It was.

Author Bio

Alexandra Melnick serves at Operation Shoestring as the Communications Director in addition to serving as the 1 Campus 1 Community Coordinator and adjunct faculty member at Millsaps College. She is an alumna of Millsaps College and the University of Mississippi, and her work has been featured in outlets such Learning for Justice, Bitterzoet, Geez Magazine, and Rewire. Alexandra is dedicated to building a better Mississippi together with her community, and lives with her husband and unruly cat Gretchen in Jackson.

Becoming

Ada Vilageliu Díaz

Reflection

During the pandemic, I created a virtual story time for my son, his school, and other children of color. I wanted to support their literacy journey through positive images of children who look like them. When we were doing online schooling, I noticed that his school Spanish textbook only had one image of a Black person, and that was to teach the word "behind." We started to color his workbooks making all the dads Black like my child's father. I was painfully reminded of the colorism and anti-Black racism in my Latinx community, and I wanted to counter those images. I wanted children like my son to read stories about BIPOC protagonists and to be encouraged to read and inspired to create their own books. The story time program ran for half a year and included weekly events with BIPOC authors reading their books to bilingual elementary school children. Children were also invited to read books and draw themselves. I created the story time with my Latinx students, who were very proud to be supporting their own communities.

We were in my son's toddler bed. He was still small enough to fit, and he liked the safety of the bed's raised sides. I had placed a small bookcase next to it so that he could build and see his book collection. As a literature instructor, I wished to get him to become a nerdy bookie like myself or at least to discover the pleasure of reading and discovering new worlds. I opened the first page of a book about the Canary Islands that I had purchased there at the last minute. As I read each page, I felt proud to pass on the book's cultural references about my homeland, but something was very wrong about this book.

We had recently returned from Tenerife in the Canary Islands to visit the family after three years of the COVID pandemic's ups and downs. We wanted to be safe, so I didn't travel during the pandemic. Spain was also on a very different pandemic schedule, and I was already too stressed out with remote work and homeschooling to even plan a trip of those proportions. However, I realized my son didn't remember his first and only visit to the island. He was too little to remember the smells, colors, sounds, sights, or even the familiar hugs. Family was reduced to facetime calls in Spanish. His English overtaking the sounds and structures of my mother tongue.

I was worried that my son would not learn how to read during virtual schooling. I felt the responsibility and the weight of having to teach him how to read in English and Spanish.

Gramma used to read to him. Each session started with the words "Read, read, read." The daily ritual of hugs in the sofa or rocking chair. Her arms around the joyful little boy, sweet and caring, arms of experience. We were each delighted to increase his vocabulary, me in Spanish, she in English. He used to call her ABCs and 123s instead of Gramma. Their bond is one of love of learning. She used to come to his playgroup classes before he got accepted into daycare, and she managed to take him to his first day in daycare before he turned two years old. A picture of her holding my son in her arms. Her smile wide like the sun.

She read to and cared for him until she died. I had to call an ambulance to take her to the hospital when I returned from teaching one of my adjunct jobs. She was laying in the sofa in pain, my son at her feet. I suspected that her stomach pain could be related to a heart attack. She had heart problems already, and I knew that women are sometimes misdiagnosed because our heart attacks could be in the jaw or the stomach. I had read that in a poster in the emergency room, and I insisted that she went to the hospital. Unlike the other times, I couldn't go with her because I had to stay home with my child. The ambulance took a very long time to pick her up. I went upstairs with my son, closed the door, and drew the curtains so my child, her only grandchild, could not see how paramedics took her out. She didn't return that night to our home by the Anacostia river. I received the call from my husband, telling me in painful gulps of air and silence. They simply said she was found dead in her room. An elderly Black woman ignored in her emergency room; her pain dismissed for hours. The darkness. The moonlight coming from the window. Silence.

Now I didn't know how to do it on my own. She was an expert educator in literacy. One of the few Black women to earn a Master's degree of her generation. How could I teach my son to read? How could I, a Spanish-speaking Latina immigrant, teach my Black child to read in English and to love himself at the same time? I was still trying to figure out my own ancestry, erased by colonial powers.

The summer I was planning my literacy project was violent. It had been violent for years. Images of Black men and women being murdered. Families and children assaulted across from the White House. I refused to watch. I knew those images from before. The pain was overwhelming. Pushed to nighttime when I could feel it, away from my child. At the same time, I had to prepare my Black son for those images and experiences. And I wished his Gramma was there to comfort all of us and teach me how to support my child. Her absence, a painful reminder that Black children need their Black family, one that we had lost to other unfortunate events.

At home, I had been building a book collection that featured children who looked like him so that I could build his self-esteem. I wanted him to feel proud of being a Black child. We had books with Black male protagonists, Black scientists, Black artists, etc. I believed that those books would counter any textbooks or content that centered whiteness. I realized that when the school sent us a Spanish textbook that didn't feature any Black images other than one Black man used to teach the word "behind." We started coloring the white Latino fathers in another Spanish workbook. I didn't feel that I could trust any school or textbook to support my son's learning through healthy images of Black children or Black people. I remembered my own educational journey and how the textbooks centered whiteness and erased the history of my islands, brutally attacked by Spanish colonizadores: gods replaced, languages erased, memories buried, while white European tourists use our home as a playground and Spaniards mock our accents. I had been struggling with my own Canary Island heritage because it had been purposely removed from my own textbooks – other than stories about flowers, animals, and volcanoes.

This book that we were reading in his small comfy bed was supposed to somewhat help me fill this gap. The Canary Islands were "discovered" in 1492 by Christopher Columbus, which led to the conquista, the enslavement, the displacement, and the whitening. I wanted to find books that included historical and cultural references about these islands so that he would feel proud. We came from warriors and survivors. We had a culture and a history before the violence. But this book we were reading was telling us that the islands were *regalos* gifted to Spain. After screaming in horror, I looked at the author's bio. The writer was from Spain and not the Canary Islands. This was the type of colonial mentality I wanted to counter. The legacy of colonialism. The legacy of Franco's dictatorship and nationalistic drive. Some books are harmful, like this one. Like the one we found at my child's school that we tossed into the trash, one with a white protagonist and a Native person who was listed as an object in a museum.

In a meeting with the Latinx students I was advising, we discussed how to start a community engagement project,and we thought of a book drive at first. The logistics were complicated during the pandemic, and we couldn't find a bookstore or library partner, so we chose to do a virtual storytime instead. We wanted to support Latinx families and provide educational content during online learning by readings bilingual books by diverse Latinx authors to their children.

The storytime we were planning had to showcase healthy and positive images of children of color. I realized that the best stories came from authors who themselves were members of those communities. At the same time, it was harder to find books published by BIPOC authors. In the case of Latinx writers, most books in Spanish were translations of books written by white authors. Most children's books also featured white protagonists or animals. I also realized that the free books we had been receiving from the Imagination Library did not include Latinx stories. We needed to showcase and celebrate the stories written by those writers who were providing joyful and complex images of BIPOC children, who were writing to and from their communities.

We created it together. My Latinx students provided me with the love and support I didn't know I needed as a Latina faculty member. Latinx administrators at my child's school and a diverse group of parents also contributed to the planning. They made me realize that the school needed more books featuring LGBTQ+ and other minority stories. I told my son that this was his story time project too, and that he was the protagonist in all of this. He was not too interested in the story time at first, and I had to convince him to sit down and pay attention to the screen when he was more excited about seeing his best friend at the virtual meetings. The authors we invited to participate were happy to support our vision. One of my Latinx students became the teaching artist and created art activities for each book. Some children would join every week, happy to listen, speak, and draw. We were also joined by other families in different states (and my own family in the island). My best friend and her daughter helped us by inviting a Native author and preparing a bead medallion activity for the children. Her daughter taught us how to draw intricate, elaborate bead medallion patterns based on her own family tradition. Her mother was holding the camera so that we could all see it in detail. After the demonstration, we all tried to draw our own versions of the bead medallion using crayons and paper at home. It was a community experience.

Our weekly meetings were a ritual of happy faces in little squares, fidgeting, listening, and jumping with joy. Many came every single Wednesday, ready to listen, engage, and draw themselves. Their smiles filled the screen, and their little hands would go up in excitement when they could ask questions to the authors themselves. They would ask very insightful questions about the creative process and the storyline. For example, one time, a small child made suggestions to Carlos Aponte on what image he could have added at the end of his book (something I can't remember right now). These children, after all, are his audience, and Carlos agreed with a huge smile that the comment made sense. There was another brilliant child who was our star reader. She would volunteer to read her favorite books at the beginning of many of our sessions, a protagonist in her own right, her expert reader's voice commanding the space. We were so enchanted by their energy, joy, and creativity that we would keep the event going until each child who wanted to speak could do so. In fact, many authors stayed until the very end to see what the children would draw and create with our teaching artists. They would proudly show their drawings and describe every little detail of their imagination. We would all cheer and celebrate their weekly creations.

And the little boy who didn't want to read started to create his own books. We would fold pages in two and create a bundle that I would staple together in the shape of a book. During story time sessions, during his own virtual class sessions, and while talking to his grandparents in Tenerife, he would draw ninjas. That was and still is my son's favorite character. In his books, he and his best friend became ninjas who fought against evil. One time, he wanted to "read" his book during a storytime event. He wanted to be the invited author. I let him show some of his pages, full of drawings, while I quickly transitioned to the guest author's reading.

I also wanted to write my own book, but I didn't know who I was. I took a virtual creative writing class with Mayra Santos Febres in Puerto Rico, who challenged me to write in Spanish and to craft my memoir, but I was only able to create fragments and images of ancestral dreams and visions. My family history on my mother's side seemed incomplete. I didn't know my roots. During a CCW fellowship opportunity with Herstory Writers, I continued to put the pieces together and tried to write my story again. I was being trained to facilitate memoir-writing sessions with communities, but my story was still stuck inside. I asked my mother to confirm my suspicion that we could be related to a Guanche warrior in the island of Tenerife. My great-grandmother's last name was Bencomo, but a clerical error and a judge decided to remove her last name from her own children's names. In the Canary Islands, we follow the Spanish model for naming. Each child gets the father's last name and the mother's last name after that. In total, everyone has two last names. When I did my family tree, an assignment I also gave to my students at Howard University as part of their reading Isabel Wilkerson's *The Warmth of Other Suns*, I found out that my mother's grandmother was named after Bencomo, the last warrior against the Spanish conquistadores. No one ever said anything to us about it. It felt part secret, part ignorance, part shame, part mystery.

When my child and I visited the Canary Islands, I made sure to share with him the story of the Guanches as his ancestors. I spent a week at the library of the Universidad de la Laguna, where I had received my BA in English and DEA (now replaced with an MA) in American literature but graduated not knowing about my own culture and heritage. At the library, my desk was full of books written by the priests and the colonizers on the one hand, and by the Canary Island researchers on the other. Stories of how ignorant, savage, and primitive we were countered by stories of how we used to pray, heal, and live before and after the conquest. It did not feel real. It still felt like I was reading about people who did not exist anymore.

It was the English Program holiday meeting and the Sigma Tau Delta English International Honor Society induction at work. I had to bring my son because the meeting was in the afternoon. We were a small group of faculty and students. I was one of the advisors to Sigma Tau Delta, and one of my students was being inducted. Other faculty, alumni, and students were joining online as we had a laptop set up on a table so that they could hear and participate. There were cookies, fruits, and drinks in this corner room surrounded by windows leading to a busy Connecticut Ave. I prepared a plate for my son and set him up with activity books, stickers, and his iPad. I wanted to keep him entertained and distracted and expected him to eat his snacks and watch Netflix while we conducted the meeting.

He stood up and introduced himself. Hi! My name is Elijah y soy descendiente de Bencomo.

Author Bio

Ada Vilageliu-Díaz received her Ph.D. in English from Howard University and her B.A. in English Philology from Universidad de La Laguna, Canary Islands. She currently teaches writing and literature courses at the University of the District of Columbia. Her research focuses on rhetoric and composition, community-based teaching, community-based scholarship, Latinx, Afro-Latinx, and Caribbean literature and writing. Her poetry has been published in Knocking on the Door of the White House: Latina and Latino Poets in Washington, D.C. In 2014, She directed the documentary Near the River about environmental women leaders in DC. During the COVID-19 Pandemic, she created--with the students of the UDC Latinx Student Association--a virtual story time featuring Latinx children's books.

I Won American Idol

Nic Nusbaumer

Reflection

When my cousins and I sang karaoke in the Carigara rice fields, we were just sounds and bodies and no money and full stomachs. Growing up, I never got to bring Pinoy home to Missouri, and *Pinoy* home always was an ocean away.

Home is a funny and unfixed thing. And, like anything that can be loved or hated, home is where we harbor a lot of our memories, space, and time. Whether home is rooted in one place, no place, or many places, we embody and live it even while we're away. I wrote this story thinking a lot about Olga Tokarczuk's *Flights* and Neisha-Anne S. Green's "The Re-Education of Neisha-Anne S. Green." Code-meshing and embodying a reflexive identity is material, rhetorical, and contextual. If you're anything, especially visibly, outside of the/a status quo, or have difficulty reconciling your histories, probably you also know what it's like to mesh into and out of some contexts–to be denied the opportunity, even. This story is about allyship, home as more than a roof over some heads, and how funny the truth can be. Because I *am* a farmer's son, and I *did* win American Idol. That's the truth!

Most people display visceral resistance when I tell them I won American Idol, perhaps confounded by the "American" part, but probably because they had no idea they were talking to a *star*.

Okay, it was my middle school's "Nixa's American Idol" competition. Where I'm from, everything is characteristically bombastic. Huge strip malls are erected but never leased. We're running out of fast-food corporations with red marketing to bid for space but are always told to "shop local" (more on that later). We have "historic downtown" everything, the only Sucker Day and Sucker Day Parade on earth, and the scraps from trends that began five years ago in other places. We like to embellish. So: I. Won. American. Idol.

After a month of auditioning in front of faculty and our hardass music teacher, Mrs. Willnauer, they chose two winners. The prize? We got to sing at Dolly Parton's *Dixie* Stampede down in Branson, which has only recently been renamed "Dolly Parton's Stampede." Without the "Dixie." You have to see it to believe it, but I'll just say: Civil War, rotisserie chicken, horses jumping through rings of fire.

"There's such a thing as innocent ignorance, and so many of us are guilty of that," Dolly said. But the show goes on.

We semi-affectionately refer to Branson as *Hillbilly Las Vegas* because that is indeed what it is. It is where people from Willard, Ozark, Rogersville, and Fair Grove–who all think Springfield is a bustling metropolis–go to "get away." It is where people from all over the world fly in to answer the questions: "No fucking shit? No way?

That. That exists?" It is where you can, in the same day, have lunch in the Titanic, see a B-list Bellagio-esque water show at the outdoor outlet mall, have second lunch at Applebee's, take a selfie with wax Michael Jackson, have first dinner somewhere nice like Ruby Tuesday, and buy a last-minute rifle for your kid's birthday.

In Branson, we have our own "strip" of dilapidated motels and once-opulent theaters showcasing ex- or wannabe Vegas performers–many of whom perform *as* famous stars like Elvis. My favorite was Yakov Smirnoff, a Ukrainian comedian who did all but tell the locals to their face how dumb he thought they were, and did so in a religiously preserved Ukrainian-English accent. We have Silver Dollar City, the most enigmatic and over-the-fucking-top amusement park in the entire world, romanticizing early settlement white plantation life in southern Missouri. Kettle corn, Bald Knobbers, and live glassblowing, *baby*. We have Ride the Ducks–closed and reopened as Branson Duck Tours–for those who've ever wondered what screaming into a duck call while driving a truck directly into the lake might be like. In 2018, sixteen passengers drowned after one such duck truck launched despite thunderstorm warnings. The show goes on. We have all the pseudo-discounted commerce and hyphenated steak the working class could ever ask for. We have manmade beaches (only men would build a fake beach next to a dam on a lake) and lots of free parking. There are mountains formed out of glacial melting and tectonic shifts, too, but yada yada let's go to Applebee's for first dinner instead of Ruby Tuesday.

Dixie Outfitters Southern Heritage Store is a mile down the road from Dolly Parton's Dixie Stampede. Since 1861, they've worked a revisionist lens into their marketing of Confederate flags, apparel, gear, and all to our local communities. They even have a short history lesson on their website, as well as a news section with anti-progressive and insurrection-apologist propaganda. The orange 1969 General Lee Charger has been parked out front since I was too short to ride Thunderation at Silver Dollar City. Car guys always say things like "Oh, man, if I had that thing, I'd do right by it." Doing right by the Lee would be painting it yellow and driving it into Table Rock lake blowing into a duck call.

"Long live Dixie!" the Dixie Outfitters president writes on the website homepage, mindlessly screenprints onto cotton. Fratboys at the private liberal arts college in Springfield yell "Long Live Dixie" when I'm home from school partying with my hometown friends. How would you rather have it? Rings of fire with a whole-half chicken or honesty?

So, like I said, I won Nixa's American Idol. It was April 2006. I was in fifth grade, chubby and cute as a tender little button. A couple months before, my parents took me on a pity cruise to ease the pain of my forthcoming knee surgery (I was a bit too chubby). I needed some holes in my knee so I could keep jumping high and throwing far. We all hated it.

My favorite stop was Aruba, where the loveliest women played with and twisted my hair into beaded braids. For many moments on that cruise, seeing my silky Asian hair jacketed in braids–protected–made me forget that I was too chubby for my own body, that leaving this hellacious cruise in the islands meant being unable to walk for two months post-op at home. I remember the ladies gossiping with my mom about how easy it was to make money off tourists at the harbor, wondering then but knowing now how beautiful it is to see your mom get to laugh about the struggle with other badass women.

We get home to Hillbilly Heaven, I win the final round of American Idol with Jet's "Look What You've Done," and I'm going to Dixie, baby! Mrs. Parsons tells me she's so proud of me. We didn't get teachers like her in Nixa: so poised, charming, altruistic. She looks and seems like young Dolly Parton, with the curliest curls, the most inviting peach tea accent, and a confident wrist flick-and-point across her torso when she knows she's right. We all loved Mrs. Parsons.

Since I was on crutches for six weeks after surgery, she took it upon herself to help me elevate my leg before she drew on transparent ELMO sheets for the class. She used to chauffeur me to and from American Idol auditions, wait for my mom with me on the sidewalk after school, and always looked me right in the eyes with the pure gloss of a badass woman who *sees* you. Even my mom loved her. Once, Mrs. Parsons told me she knew what it was like to feel invisible even when you see yourself so clearly, even when your mom raised you damn good.

We all loved Mrs. Parsons.

I needed a song for Dixie Stampede. It was killing me. Between missing an entire season of baseball (i.e., delaying the only thing that bonded my dad and me back then), enduring the weird interactions around my crutches and fucky leg, and the anxiety of looking like *this* while singing in front of a crowd of cowboys and gals, even my cool beaded braids took a backseat to the fuckery. In fifth grade, the Black Eyed Peas were *huge*; like, "Where is the Love?" and "Let's Get it [Started]" huge. Mom's best quirk has always been telling me mainstream celebrities are Filipino, and when I found out that Black Eyed Peas' member Allan Pineda Lindo (APL) is not only Filipino but that BEP had a song in *Tagalog,* it was easy: I'd sing "The APL Song."

But, I was afraid singing in Tagalog would be too weird, maybe even too proud, that maybe I should pump the brakes and just sing something purely American. "Louisiana Woman, Mississippi Man." Mom reminded me how much I laughed when I sang karaoke with my cousins in the Philippines; how little I cared then. I felt my toes strapped into thong flip-flops and remembered what it was like to sing into the silent jungle. Like water under a bag of tea, Mrs. Parsons supports me, too, reminds me I'm already on crutches, that I've already won. She could've just said, "Have you *seen* your hair?" This was an experiment in having just enough power and just enough privilege and just enough positionality to make weird work. It was getting to use my language in *my* voice. I got to use *my* chubby brown body to sing about *my* Pinoy people in a place that thrives on censure and forgetting. That way, they can't forget.

That is the fucking American dream.

Mom cried the first time I hit the chorus in rehearsals, a second time after I got to sing at Dixie Stampede:

Lapit mga kaibigan
At makinig kayo

Ako'y may dala-dalang balita galing sa bayan ko
Nais kong ipamahagi ang mga kwento
At mga pangayaring nagaganap sa lupang 'pinangako

[listen closely, everyone, I have news for my hometown. I want to share what's going on in the so-called "promised land"]

I got all the shine from my friends and classmates, ate my rotisserie chicken, and humbly fell down the stairs after the show because Branson is somehow nicer to Asian bodies than temporarily disabled ones. I missed a step with my crutches and toppled over gracefully. The guttural gasps of everyone around me were simply mouthwatering. Surely I was more broken than before. Mrs. Dolly Parsons' curls cut into the frame. Mom was stunned, but they both laugh when I do. They set me right and got my crutches back under me. Nothing hurt. I won American Idol, who gives a shit!

Author Bio

Nic Nusbaumer (he/him) is a Filipino American writer raised in Nixa, Missouri who enjoys cycling, Magic: The Gathering, hardcore punk, and jasmine rice. He is also a Writing and Rhetoric PhD student at George Mason University, studying institutional ethnography and the rhetoric of education policy. This year, Nic is a Jacob Volkman Human Rights Fellow with Herstory Foundation.

SpeakOut! CLC

Constance Davis, Grace Dotson, Mia Manfredi, Ainhoa Palacios, and Tanya Sopkin, with Tobi Jacobi and Mary Ellen Sanger

Reflection

Five interns at the Community Literacy Center at Colorado State University (Mia Manfredi, Constance Davis, Tanya Sopkin, Ainhoa Palacios, and Grace Dotson) collaborated in the creation of this piece (with guidance and a few words from the directors, Tobi Jacobi and Mary Ellen Sanger). Each of us has participated within a cluster of SpeakOut! writing workshops over the course of the fall 2022 semester, which take place at shelters for the unhoused, rehabilitation centers, and community correction/work release facilities. Each of our experiences is vastly different, though we noticed similar themes arising within our group discussions about the individual workshops. Elements of comfort, vulnerability, imagination, curiosity, diversity, and individualism are significant components within the program. SpeakOut! allows us to transcend our preconceived notions of creativity, reaching others with a collective voice from a heightened platform.

The piece began with a close look at lines compiled from free writing we did individually and then as a group, as we wrote and shared our experiences about facilitating SpeakOut! workshops. We turned segments of those responses into this poem. We began to write the final version with inspiration from Ocean Vuong's novel, *On Earth We're Briefly Gorgeous*. Within his book, the narrator alternates between sections of poetic lines that capture feelings and reflections, and then he braids those lines with narration of specific memories. Using a similar style, we combined the emotions that arose before, during, and after workshops with specific memories and recollections of the workshops.

Learn more about the CLC's work at https://literacy.colostate.edu/ and the SpeakOut! Writing Workshops that inspired this piece at https://speakoutclc.wordpress.com/.

SpeakOut, lingering

1. *Uncertainty*

I'm nervous
    until I am not.
Am I the only one who feels this way?

A woman walks into the space

and grabs onto the door frame.
She says, "I've never written a poem,"
but enters, anyway.

I'm nervous
        at first.
Then elated when more start to join.

I'm nervous
        until each of us reaches for a pen.

We collectively begin to
enjoy each other's company.

**Sometimes I think I have to be on top of everything—but most of the time every-
thing falls into place perfectly as it should be.**

• *Write about trust in yourself.*

2.   *I become vulnerable*

Writing spaces can be intimidating.
A place to confront the past and the future
by creating in the present.

The retelling of memories
through vulnerable work.

This process is aided by having a certain level of
        softness.

Creating, sharing
        beautiful, raw emotions.

I am almost at a loss for words.

**Sometimes writers read aloud. Many of their words come from a vul-
nerable space. They seem hesitant about the responses that may come.**

However, after each participant shares with the group, writers engage in uplifting, supportive conversations with one another about their writing. Feelings of empathy and admiration spread throughout the room.

- *Write about a time you felt empowered.*

3. *Comfort*

I want them to feel comfortable to
　　　express,
comfortable to share.
A space for wonder and exploration
　　　maybe, wandering aimlessly–
For processing with others around us
For pushing through the weeds & roadblocks of the day
Moving towards places where words wait for selection
A safer space
A gateway to creativity, honesty, risks, imagination and confidence.

I want to make the women feel comfortable, and I myself want to feel comfortable. We usually have a few new writers each time, and every one of them brings her own unique ideas to chat, think, and write about. Within each workshop, I attempt to make each writer feel comfortable expressing whatever those things may be.

- *Write about a time you wandered with intention.*

4. *SpeakOut!*
your mind.
Unleash your thoughts.
Tell us what we have been dying to hear,

Your voice.

We write about someone we love,

about our siblings,

about those who have hurt us.

We become so engrossed in what we're writing.

We tell the writers to come as they are, to write as they wish, to read what they'd like. Maybe I'd like to do that as well.

- *Write about a time when your voice was heard/felt powerful.*

5. *Share*

their voice, their stories.
Some days they are timid,
shy.

Then, the group applauds,
taken away by their words.

Here we are, in a sacred space.

I could see thoughts churning in everyone. We sat in silence for some time. It was an agreed-upon and necessary silence where every writer and facilitator mulled an idea we may have never had before— or not for a long time.

- *Write about a time you enjoyed silence.*

6. *…to linger on words…*

All that was created in one hour did not exist before.

When our time ends, everyone lingers, talking about their future writing plans, sharing stories, discussing ideas for next week. The time goes by so fast, I feel like I am never ready for it to end. I walk to my car, the words falling away from me briskly as the other parts of life flood back in: *Who has homework? Are the dishes done? Who needs picking up? What did I forget today?*

I hold my notebook, wanting to linger.

Write.

***

Author Bios

Constance Davis is a graduate of Colorado State University with a major in Ethnic Studies and a concentration in Sociology. She has expanded her skills of critical analysis in psychology and criminal justice, where her interests are most prevalent.

Grace Dotson is a senior sociology and criminology major at Colorado State University. She became involved with the Community Literacy Center at CSU when she started as a volunteer for Speakout! in the Spring of 2022 at the Fort Collins Mission. Since then, she has been an intern for the community literacy center and facilitated creative writing workshops at AspenRidge recovery center. Grace has cherished her time meeting writers and building community through writing in the Fort Collins area. Grace feels passionate that creative work fosters empathy and understanding and plans to continue work that centers on uplifting the voices and stories of others throughout her life.

Tobi Jacobi and **Mary Ellen Sanger** direct the Community Literacy Center in the English Department at Colorado State University. The CLC's mission remains focused on creating and facilitating literacy opportunities that invite community members to engage in innovative and supportive writing spaces and to value the writing and art that emerges through conversation and circulation

Mia Manfredi is a fourth-year student at Colorado State University. She has a major in English with a concentration in Creative Writing and a minor in Sociology. Mia is an aspiring activist, artist, and writer. She enjoys writing and reading YA fiction, painting, drawing, collaging, and volunteering within her community. She is very passionate about women's rights, educational equity, environmental justice, and economic justice!

Ainhoa Palacios is a fiction candidate in the MFA program at Colorado State University, as well as a graduate teacher for the English department. She enjoys writing fiction, and creative nonfiction and has been published in journals like Lumiere Review,

Somos En Escrito, and *Sunspot Literary Journal*. Her stories are often themed around Latinx characters, and the displacement commonly felt by immigrants and children of immigrants.

Tanya Sopkin is a second-year student at Colorado State University studying Sociology and a minor in English. Their works have been published in CSU's Literary Magazines *Spiritus Mundi* and *The Greyrock Review*, as well as the University of New Mexico's Literary Journal *Scribendi*. They love reading, blogging about TV shows and queer issues, and plan to go into Social Work after graduating.

PARLOR PRESS

EQUIPMENT FOR LIVING

Now with Parlor Press!

Studies in Rhetorics and Feminism
   Series Editors: Cheryl Glenn and Shirley Wilson Logan

Emerging Conversations in the Global Humanities
   Series Editor: Victor E. Taylor

The X-Series
   Series Editor: Jordan Frith

New Releases

Reimagining the Humanities, edited by Barry Mauer and Anastasia Salter

Global Rhetorical Traditions, edited by Hui Wu and Tarez Samra Graban

Rhetorical Listening in Action: A Concept-Tacticc Approach by Krista Ratcliffe and Kyle Jensen

A Rhetoric of Becoming: USAmerican Women in Qatar by Nancy Small

Emotions and Affect in Writing Centers, edited by Janine Morris and Kelly Concannon

MLA Mina Shaughnessy Prize and CCCC Best Book Award 2021!

Creole Composition: Academic Writing and Rhetoric in the Anglophone Caribbean, edited by Vivette Milson-Whyte, Raymond Oenbring, and Brianne Jaquette

Check Out Our New Website!

Discounts, blog, open access titles, instant downloads, and more.

www.parlorpress.com

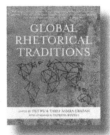

CLJ **Discount:** Use CLJ20 at checkout to receive a 20% discount on all titles not on sale through September 1, 2023.